Yves Engler is a political activist and author of twelve books. He has been dubbed as "one of the most important voices on the Canadian Left." *The Globe and Mail* has situated him in the mould of I.F. Stone, while Quill & Quire says Engler is "part of that rare but growing group of social critics unafraid to confront Canada's self-satisfied myths." Yves Engler lives in Montreal.

Owen Schalk is a writer from Manitoba. He is the author of *Canada in Afghanistan: A Story of Military, Diplomatic, Political, and Media Failure, 2003-2023* (Lorimer Books, 2023). His articles have been published by *Alborada, Monthly Review, and Protean Magazine*, and he contributes a weekly column to Canadian Dimension magazine. His fiction has appeared in *Quagmire Literary Magazine, Sobotka Literary Magazine*, Vast Chasm Magazine, and more.

Rob Rolfe is the author of seven books of poetry and three poetry chapbooks. His poetry has appeared in many Canadian journals, and in poetry anthologies in Canada and the United States. Rob was a librarian and union leader in Toronto and has served as Owen Sound Poets Laureate with singer-songwriter Larry Jensen.

T0248259

**CANADA'S LONG FIGHT
AGAINST DEMOCRACY**

CANADA'S LONG FIGHT AGAINST DEMOCRACY

Yves Engler and Owen Schalk

Baraka
Books

Montréal

© Yves Engler and Owen Schalk
© Rob Rolfe for poems on pages 101, 148, 153. First published in *Don't Look Back: Poems, Prose, Songs* (The Ginger Press, 2023)

ISBN 978-1-77186-342-1 pbk 978-1-77186-351-3;
epub 978-1-77186-352-0 pdf

Cover by Maison 1608
Book Design by Folio Infographie
Editing and proofreading: Robin Philpot, Anne Marie Marko

Legal Deposit, 1st quarter 2024
Bibliothèque et Archives nationales du Québec
Library and Archives Canada

Published by Baraka Books of Montreal

Printed and bound in Quebec

Trade Distribution & Returns
Canada – UTP Distribution: UTPdistribution.com

United States
Independent Publishers Group: IPGbook.com

We acknowledge the support from the Société de développement des entreprises culturelles (SODEC) and the Government of Quebec tax credit for book publishing administered by SODEC.

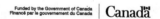

CONTENTS

Introduction   1
Iran, 1953   9
Colombia, 1953   14
Guatemala, 1954   16
The Democratic Republic of the Congo, 1961   20
The Dominican Republic, 1963   33
Brazil, 1964   39
Indonesia, 1965   43
Ghana, 1966   47
Greece, 1967   54
Uganda, 1971   58
Chile, 1973   63
Peru, 1992   69
Russia, 1993   72
Haiti, 2004   76
Palestine, 2006   102
Honduras, 2009   106
Paraguay, 2012   117
Ukraine, 2014   122
Brazil, 2016   136
Bolivia, 2019   139
Peru, 2022   149
Venezuela, 2017 to the present   154

Conclusion   171
Notes   181

INTRODUCTION

Canada supports democracy around the world. The leaders of this country promote free and fair elections, freedom of assembly, and freedom of the press.

At least, that's what Canadian officials say. Lester B. Pearson waxed eloquent about "the struggle of free, expanding progressive democracy against tyrannical and reactionary communism."[1] Pierre Trudeau lauded "the freedom of individuals and of nations, the political freedom which distinguishes East from West."[2]

To justify Canada's 2004 intervention in Haiti, Prime Minister Martin talked about the primacy of democracy to economic development while Stephen Harper's foreign affairs minister John Baird declared that "Canada will continue to support people who are seeking to bring freedom, democracy, human rights and the rule of law to their respective countries."[3] In 2019 foreign affairs minister Chrystia Freeland claimed Canada supported Ukraine since the country was at the "forefront of the struggle between democracy and authoritarianism," while a 2021 release from Justin Trudeau was titled "Prime Minister focuses on protecting democracy at Summit for Democracy."[4]

Alongside the pro-democracy rhetoric, the federal government has instigated various initiatives with the ostensible aim of promoting democracy. In 1988, the

Brian Mulroney government set up the International Centre for Human Rights and Democratic Development (Rights and Democracy). In 2009, Harper opened a South America-focused "democracy promotion" centre at the embassy in Peru while the Canada Fund for Local Initiatives, a financing mechanism overseen by diplomatic outposts, lists "democracy" as a top concern.

Echoing government officials, the media regularly suggests Canada seeks to promote democracy. They frame conflicts with countries ranging from China to Russia to Iran as motivated by a belief in democracy.

At the more critical end of the mainstream discussion, commentators sometimes complain that Ottawa does business with or maintains ties to undemocratic regimes. In the years before this book went to print, there was significant criticism of Canada selling light armoured vehicles to Saudi Arabia. In an earlier period, there was some criticism of Canada's ties to Hosni Mubarak in Egypt and Suharto in Indonesia as well as Ferdinand Marcos in the Philippines, Duvalier in Haiti and the shah in Iran. There is, in fact, an underexplored history of Canadian officials supporting autocratic and repressive regimes. But this book is not about Canada accommodating to an unjust world by passively/actively supporting dictatorships.

Rather, it is about Ottawa passively/actively subverting elected governments around the world and why it has done so.

Canada has repeatedly endorsed US-backed military coups against elected, usually progressive, leaders.

As we will show, Canada has passively supported the ouster of, or actively contributed to, the overthrow of at least twenty elected governments. Ottawa passively supported the removal of Iranian prime minister Mohammad Mossadegh in 1953, Guatemalan president Jacobo Árbenz in 1954, Dominican Republic leader Juan Bosch in 1963, Brazilian president João Goulart in 1964, Indonesian president Sukarno in 1966, Ugandan president Milton Obote in 1971, Paraguayan leader Fernando Lugo in 2012, Brazilian leader Dilma Rousseff in 2016, and Peruvian president Pedro Castillo in 2022. Additionally, Canada offered quiet support to military interventions that impeded progressive leaders in Colombia and Greece in 1953 and 1967 as well as 'coups' by presidents against their parliaments in Peru and Russia in 1992 and 1993.

In a more substantial contribution to undermining electoral democracy, Ottawa backed the Chilean military removing elected president Salvador Allende in 1973. From economic asphyxiation to diplomatic isolation, Ottawa's policy towards Allende's Chile was clear. Within three weeks of the coup, Canada recognized Pinochet's military junta and immediately after that Canada's ambassador to Chile cabled External Affairs that Pinochet "has assumed the probably thankless task of sobering Chile up" from "the riffraff of the Latin American Left to whom Allende gave asylum."

Ottawa backed the Honduran military's removal of elected president Manuel Zelaya. Before his 2009 ouster, Canadian officials criticized Zelaya and afterwards condemned his attempts to return to the country. Failing to suspend its military training program with Honduras, Canada was also the only major donor to Honduras— the largest recipient of Canadian assistance in Central America—that failed to sever any aid to the military government. Six months after the coup, Ottawa endorsed an electoral farce and immediately recognized the new right-wing government.

In a similar degree of involvement, Ottawa supported the 2019 ouster of Bolivia's first Indigenous president. Hours after the military command forced Evo Morales to resign, foreign affairs minister Chrystia Freeland released a celebratory statement declaring, "Canada stands with Bolivia and the democratic will of its people." Ottawa also provided significant support for the Organization of American States' effort to discredit Bolivia's 2019 vote, which fueled opposition protests and justified the coup.

Ottawa worked to subvert Palestinians' democratic vote in 2006. After Hamas won that year's legislative elections, Canada imposed sanctions against the Palestinians. Ottawa's aid cut-off and refusal to recognize a Palestinian unity government helped spur fighting between Hamas and Fatah, ending a short-lived electoral experiment.

In the 1960s, Ottawa played a substantial role in the ouster of pan-Africanist independence leaders Kwame Nkrumah and Patrice Lumumba. In 1966, Ghana's Canadian-trained army overthrew Nkrumah. In an internal memo to External Affairs just after

Nkrumah was ousted, Canadian high commissioner in Accra, C.E. McGaughey, wrote "a wonderful thing has happened for the West in Ghana and Canada has played a worthy part." Soon after the coup, Ottawa informed the military junta that Canada intended to carry on normal relations and Canada sent $1.82 million ($15 million today) worth of flour to Ghana.

Through its important role in a UN mission to the Congo, Ottawa contributed greatly to independence leader Patrice Lumumba's demise. Canadian colonel Jean Berthiaume assisted the elected prime minister's enemies recapturing him and soon after Lumumba was killed. Canadian officials celebrated the demise of an individual that prime minister John Diefenbaker privately called a "major threat to Western interests."

Between 2010 and 2014, Canada waged a campaign to subvert an elected government in Ukraine. At the start of the three-month Maidan uprising that toppled president Viktor Yanukovych, foreign affairs minister John Baird attended an anti-government rally in Kyiv. Ottawa also implemented sanctions on the Yanukovych government and Maidan activists used the Canadian Embassy as a safe haven for a week. Furthermore, Ottawa quickly recognized the post-coup government despite having sent election observers to monitor the 2010 presidential and 2012 parliamentary elections, which were won by Yanukovych and his Party of Regions.

Canada most aggressively subverted a progressive elected government in the Western Hemisphere's most impoverished nation. On January 31 and February 1, 2003, Jean Chrétien's Liberal government organized an international gathering to discuss overthrowing Haiti's democratically-elected president Jean-Bertrand Aristide. No Haitian officials were invited to the "Ottawa Initiative on Haiti," where high-level US, Canadian, and French officials decided Aristide "must go," the army should be re-created and the country put under UN trusteeship.

Thirteen months after the "Ottawa Initiative on Haiti" meeting, Aristide and most other elected officials were pushed out and a quasi-UN trusteeship had begun. Canadian special forces "secured" the airport from which Aristide was bundled ("kidnapped" in his words) onto a plane by US Marines and deposited in the Central African Republic. Five hundred Canadian troops occupied Haiti for the next six months.

Similar in scope to Ottawa's subversion of democracy in Haiti, the Justin Trudeau government openly sought to overthrow Venezuela's government. In a bid to elicit "regime change," Ottawa worked to isolate Caracas, imposed illegal sanctions, took that government to the International Criminal Court, financed an often-unsavoury opposition, and decided a marginal opposition politician was the legitimate president. Indeed, the same day Juan Guaidó declared himself president of Venezuela in a Caracas park, foreign affairs minister Chrystia Freeland formally recognized the little-known opposition politician. Additionally, Canadian diplomats played an important role in uniting large swaths of the Venezuelan opposition, as well as international forces, behind a plan to proclaim as president the new head of the opposition-dominated National Assembly. Unlike the other cases, Ottawa's remarkable multi-year campaign to subvert the Venezuelan government failed.

Washington's role in subverting elected governments has been detailed in countless studies by scholars and observers from around the world. The literature on Canada's role in anti-democratic meddling is comparatively limited. In fact, this is the first book to focus solely on Canada's role in subverting democracy around the globe.

IRAN, 1953

In 1953, the US and Britain overthrew Iran's first popularly elected prime minister, Mohammad Mossadegh. Mossadegh was a nationalist politician who believed the country's natural resources, particularly its large oil reserves, should be controlled by Iranians rather than Western companies. With the Louis St. Laurent government's quiet support, Mossadegh was removed in a CIA-engineered coup and replaced by shah Reza Pahlavi, who helmed a brutal regime for nearly three decades.

In the lead-up to the 1953 coup against Mossadegh, the British Embassy in Tehran represented Canada's diplomatic relations in the country. During these years files concerning Iran at Canada's Department of External Affairs largely consisted of US and British reports, but Canadian officials still voiced their disapproval of Mossadegh and his policies. Thirteen months before the coup, Canada's ambassador in Washington cabled Ottawa: "The situation in Iran could hardly look worse than it does at present. Mossadegh has been returned to power with increased influence and prestige and will almost certainly prove even more unreasonable and intractable than in the past, so that a settlement of the oil dispute will be harder than ever to arrange."[1]

Mossadegh's supposed intractability stemmed from the fact that he wanted Iranians to benefit from the country's huge oil reserves. The British had different plans. As one of the earliest sources of Middle Eastern oil, the Anglo-Iranian Oil Company (British Petroleum's predecessor) had generated immense wealth for British investors since 1915. Unwilling to yield any of its profits, Anglo-Iranian chairman Sir William Fraser responded to Iran's attempts to gain a greater share of its oil wealth by proclaiming "one penny more and the company goes broke."[2] Yet a 1952 State Department report showed the company was selling its oil at between ten and thirty times its production cost.[3] Needless to say, Anglo-Iranian Oil was unpopular. Even the US State Department noted the company's "arrogance had made it genuinely hated in Iran."[4] In the face of Anglo-Iranian intransigence, Mossadegh defied London and supported the nationalization of the country's oil industry. It was a historic move that made Iran the first former colony to reclaim its oil.

Ottawa was not happy with the Iranian government's move. In May 1951, external affairs minister Lester Pearson told the House of Commons the "problem can be settled" only if the Iranians keep in mind the "legitimate interests of other people who have ministered to the well-being of Iran in administering the oil industry of that country which they have been instrumental in developing."[5] Later that year Pearson complained about the Iranians' "emotional" response to the English. He added: "In their anxiety to gain full control of their affairs by the elimination of foreign influence, they are exposing themselves to the menace of communist penetration and absorption—absorption into the Soviet sphere."[6]

Notwithstanding Pearson's warning, Mossadegh was a secular nationalist, not a communist, and his relationship with the Soviet Union was limited. As Mossadegh biographer Farhad Diba explains, "the Soviet attitude towards the Mossadegh Government vacillated between a 'hands-off' policy and the maintenance of correct but politely distant relations."[7] When Mossadegh began making moves to reclaim Iran's resources from Western business interests, the Soviets praised his anti-imperialism, but made few moves to deepen cooperation with his government.

In response to Mossadegh's oil nationalization, the British government organized an embargo of Iranian oil, which Ottawa followed.[8] The embargo weakened Mossadegh's government, enabling the CIA's subsequent drive to topple the nationalist prime minister.

Following a meeting of the National Security Council on March 11, 1953, head of the CIA Allan Dulles gave the agency's Tehran bureau one million US dollars ($8 million today) to be used "in any way that would bring about the fall of Mossadegh."[9] In *All the Shah's Men*, Stephen Kinzer explains: "Through a variety of means, covert agents would manipulate public opinion and turn as many Iranians as possible against Mossadegh. This effort, for which $150,000 was budgeted, would 'create, extend and enhance public hostility and distrust and fear of Mossadegh and his government.' It would portray Mossadegh as corrupt, pro-communist, hostile to Islam, and bent on destroying the morale and readiness of the armed forces. While Iranian agents spread these lies, thugs would be paid to launch staged attacks on religious leaders and make it appear that they were ordered by Mossadegh or his supporters."[10]

Pearson did not protest the overthrow of Iran's first elected prime minister. Privately, External Affairs celebrated. Three days after Mossadegh was ousted, a cable from the ambassador in Washington explained: "Perhaps the most disturbing and unpredictable factor [in Iran] was the continued strength of the Tudeh party."[11] Iran's Communist Party, Tudeh, pushed for the nationalization of the Anglo-Iranian Oil Company and its support for Mossadegh was used to justify the coup. External Affairs joined Anglo-American efforts to demonize and criminalize Tudeh by sending the RCMP a copy of a UK government report titled the "Tudeh Party of Persia."[12]

When some Canadians asked External Affairs "to prevent the imprisonment or execution of premier Mossadegh of Iran," they were told nothing could be done.[13] Four months after the coup, Canada's ambassador in Washington cabled Ottawa about "encouraging reports from their [US] embassy in Tehran on the growing strength of the present [coup] government."[14] Two years after Mossadegh's illegal overthrow, Canada began diplomatic relations with Iran.[15] In 1965, the shah visited Ottawa, where he was taken to Parliament and welcomed at a reception party hosted by governor general Georges Vanier. Ottawa supported the extremely unpopular Pahlavi, who purchased $60 million ($600 million today) in Canadian weapons in the 1970s, until his overthrow in the nationwide revolution of 1979.[16]

Canada played a small but noteworthy role in overthrowing Iranian democracy in 1953.

COLOMBIA, 1953

In June 1953, Gustavo Rojas Pinilla seized power. Colombia's political establishment backed the general's coup, hoping Rojas would end the rural insurgencies that erupted after the assassination of Liberal leader Jorge Eliécer Gaitán. *La Violencia*, which saw left-wing guerrillas rise up against the entrenched conservative government, resulted in 13,000 deaths in 1952 alone.[1]

General Rojas took a hardline position against the guerrillas. He sought to "eradicate the roots of communism [through] his brutal use of force."[2] Ottawa ignored Rojas's violent attacks against peasants and democracy activists. In fact, the Canadian government pushed for greater commercial cooperation with the dictatorial regime and Rojas was praised by the press. In "Securing the Expansion of Capitalism in Colombia: Canadair and the Military Regime of General Gustavo Rojas Pinilla (1953–1957)," Stefano Tijerina writes, "the Canadian government also welcomed the military dictatorship. The *Winnipeg Free Press*, for example, pointed out the peaceful transition of power after the military coup, paying minimal attention to the violation of the democratic process in Colombia. Six months after the military coup, the Alberta daily newspaper, *The Medicine Hat News*, presented a very favourable view of General Rojas, describing him as the 'leader' that brought 'law and order' back to the country. The West had given legitimacy to the military regime; Western nations believed in his nation-building project, and more specifically, in his commitment to eradicating communism."[3]

During the Rojas dictatorship, the Canadian government secured the sale of six Canadair F-86 fighter jets to the repressive regime. According to Tijerina, "the transaction marked the first sale of Canadian jet aircraft to Latin America and the first time a deal of this kind occurred outside NATO and the Commonwealth."[4]

In discussing the sale, government officials noted privately that the fighter jets would be useful to "suppress revolt" in Rojas's Colombia.[5] In arguing in favour of selling the arms, external affairs minister Lester Pearson pointed to the benefits for the Canadian aircraft industry and that Colombia "was the best friend that Canada had in South America and it would be difficult to explain why the export of the aircraft could not be permitted."[6] He added that securing the sale with Rojas would open the door for other Canadian companies to profit in Colombia.

Popular protests prompted the Colombian elite to remove Rojas from power in May 1957, but the general laid the groundwork for Colombia's twentieth-century economic liberalization. Canadian corporations greatly benefitted from these policies.[7]

GUATEMALA, 1954

In 1953, the CIA launched Operation PBSUCCESS to overthrow Guatemalan president Jacobo Árbenz. The covert action agency conducted an extensive propaganda campaign to undermine Árbenz, which included promoting a Guatemalan "liberation army" established in Honduras. Under the command of exiled army officer colonel Carlos Castillo Armas, this small military force coordinated their attacks with the CIA. As part of these efforts, the US Navy enforced a sea blockade of Guatemala while US warplanes buzzed Guatemala City to sow popular panic and dissent within the army. In the face of this onslaught, Guatemala's elected president stepped down and a series of military men took his place. Ottawa welcomed the military coup and Canadian investment in Guatemala increased in subsequent years.

In 1944, a popular uprising in Guatemala overthrew the US-backed military dictatorship of Jorge Ubico and led to free elections in which Juan José Arévalo, a left-of-centre nationalist, became Guatemala's first democratically-elected leader. Arévalo implemented modest reforms favouring the dispossessed, including the Maya who the Spanish nearly wiped out to establish a settler-plantation economy. In the early 1900s, US-based fruit producers, notably the United

Fruit Company, began to dominate Guatemala's economy. Famous American-Canadian railroad baron Sir William Van Horne helped the United Fruit Company build the railway required to export bananas from the country.

Arévalo's reforms were popular among ordinary Guatemalans, but they irked the domestic landed class, US business interests, and Washington. Jacobo Árbenz's 1950 election, with 65% of the vote, convinced the elite and Washington that they must put a stop to the social democratic reforms.

Following in the footsteps of Arévalo, Árbenz prioritized rural agrarian reform, targeting the unproductive holdings of large companies. Washington screamed communism, but Árbenz was not a proto-Castro. As Eduardo Galeano pointed out, Árbenz drew "his inspiration not from Lenin but from Abraham Lincoln. His agrarian reform, an attempt to modernize Guatemala capitalism, [was] less radical than the North American rural laws of almost a century ago."[1]

Árbenz ran afoul of Washington decision-makers when he gave landless peasants uncultivated land owned by the United Fruit Company (the Boston-based company was offered compensation at the price they valued the property for tax purposes). "By far the largest property owner in the country," 85% of United Fruit's 550,000 acres of land was unused in 1953.[2] The company had monopolized Guatemala's banana exports, its telephone and telegraph facilities as well as its main Atlantic harbour and nearly every mile of railroad track in the country.[3] Long-time United Fruit employee, Thomas McCann, summarized the company's history in Guatemala: "Guatemala was chosen as the site of the company's earliest development activities at the turn of the century because a good portion of the country contained prime banana land and because at the time we entered Central America, Guatemala's government was the region's weakest, most corrupt and most pliable. In short, the country offered an 'ideal investment climate,' and United Fruit's profits there flourished for fifty years. Then something went wrong: a man named Jacobo Árbenz became president."[4]

Beyond United Fruit, Washington worried that Árbenz's social democratic policies would disrupt the elite-dominated status quo in the region. In 1954, a State Department official was unusually blunt, pointing out that "Guatemala has become an increasing threat to the stability of Honduras and El Salvador. Its agrarian reform is a powerful propaganda weapon; its broad social program of aiding the workers and peasants in a victorious struggle against the upper classes and large foreign enterprises has a strong appeal to the populations of Central American neighbors where similar conditions prevail."[5] Árbenz represented the threat of a bad example.

Prior to Árbenz's election, Canada's trade commissioner in Guatemala had described him as "unscrupulous, daring and ruthless, and not one to be allayed in his aims by bloodshed or killing."[6] He concluded that "businessmen and landowners do not have any cause to view the prospect of Arbenz as future president with any optimism."[7]

Canada helped isolate Árbenz . With the US seeking to de-stabilize his government, Árbenz sought to demonstrate that Guatemala had cordial relations with a US ally and was not a threat. But Ottawa refused the request to open embassies in each other's countries in 1953 and again in 1954.[8]

Despite opposition questioning by the CCF in the House, Pearson refused to acknowledge US involvement in the invasion of Guatemala. He said: "To the best of my knowledge, based on information we have received, the attacking forces in Guatemala seem to be Guatemalan, though some non-Guatemalans might be included."[9] Canada's external affairs minister admitted that he had foreknowledge that "matters" in Guatemala "would be reaching a climax very shortly," but claimed not to know what would bring the situation to a head.[10]

In *Northern Shadows: Canadians in Central America*, Peter McFarlane summarizes: "At External Affairs and in Canadian [corporate] boardrooms, the coup [against Árbenz] was chalked up as another victory of the Free World against the [Soviet] Menace."[11]

But the coup was a "definitive blow to Guatemala's young democracy." Árbenz's successor, Castillo Armas, immediately outlawed peasant organizations and unions and reversed the previous ten years of agrarian reform. The coup led to a series of dictatorships and a three decade long civil war that cost more than 100,000 lives.[12]

THE DEMOCRATIC REPUBLIC
OF THE CONGO, 1961

The Canadian military played a significant role in the overthrow of Patrice Lumumba, the first prime minister of the Democratic Republic of the Congo. In the final days of a hastily organized independence, the Congolese elected the strident anti-colonialist Lumumba, who was once imprisoned by the Belgians. After his election, he sought to implement his vision of an independent, decolonized, pan-Africanist Congo, which earned the ire of Belgian, US, and Canadian officials. Lumumba would only be prime minister for 81 days before foreign forces and domestic enemies organized his murder.

The political forces galvanized by Lumumba threatened Belgium's plan to maintain control over the newly independent country's resources and, in particular, the behemoth Union Minière mining company. To undermine the elected prime minister, the former colonial power backed a secessionist movement in the eastern Katanga province and supported a coup and Lumumba's assassination. During this time Ottawa was a willing partner in Belgian/US policy.

The Belgians oversaw a particularly oppressive colonial regime in the Congo. They largely excluded

Africans from higher education and professional positions, while foreign corporations pillaged its natural resources.[1] A number of Canadian companies had a vested interest in maintaining the colonial system in the Congo and throughout Africa.

But Lumumba allied with Ghanaian president Kwame Nkrumah on an alliance in the hopes of developing independent African states "with a view to liberating the whole continent of Africa from colonialism and imperialism."[2] The two leaders drafted a secret agreement for a "Union of African States," which would be based in Léopoldville, renamed Kinshasa in 1966. Additionally, Lumumba's openness to cooperating with the Soviet Union to achieve his objectives seemed to confirm the worst fears of Western ruling classes.

UN officials openly scorned Lumumba's independence-minded domestic and foreign policy. Canadian prime minister John Diefenbaker supported UN secretary-general Dag Hammarskjöld's anti-Lumumba line. "In government decisions and speeches," writes Diefenbaker aide H. Basil Robinson, "he did what he could to bring support to [Hammarskjöld]."[3] Diefenbaker supported a separatist movement in the Katanga province to destabilize the Congolese leader's fledgling administration.[4]

Twelve days after independence, the resource rich eastern province of Katanga declared independence. Union Minière immediately began paying tax to the secessionist government rather than the proper legal authority in Kinshasa. That payment totalled 70%

of Katanga's entire budget.[5] While Washington and UN officials pressed Lumumba to request a UN force to quell social disturbances in the Western capital city of Kinshasa, Lumumba ultimately asked for an international force to halt a rebellion in the east of the country.

Nearly 2,000 Canadian troops served in the Organisation des Nations Unies au Congo (ONUC) despite Congolese authorities' reservations about their participation. Lumumba expressed a desire for "considerations of nationality and race" in the UN force, which was ignored by Canadian officials who were themselves quite race conscious.[6] According to internal files unearthed by Kevin A. Spooner at Wilfrid Laurier University, military officers were concerned about Canadian troops living with "the native troops serving under United Nations."

While Lumumba never openly argued that Canadian soldiers were undesirable, Soviet officials did. Prior to their deployment, the Soviet Union's ambassador to the UN, Vasily Kuznetsov, explained: "Canada is a member of the NATO military block which also includes Belgium which has committed an aggression against the independent Congo. In these conditions the dispatch of Canadian troops, or of troops of any other state belonging to a military bloc of which Belgium is a member, would constitute nothing but assistance to the aggressor from his military ally."[7]

Canadian archives suggest Moscow's criticism wasn't far from the mark. In a private exchange, external affairs minister Howard Green told the Belgian ambassador that Ottawa "would do all [it] could [through its role in ONUC] to avoid making the situation more difficult for the Belgian government."[8] *A Role for Canada in an African Crisis* explains how Ottawa "shaped policy in a manner that offered some support for Belgian actions. They were consistently concerned with the impact of Canadian policy on their [NATO] ally."[9]

Nineteen hundred mostly French-speaking Canadian troops participated in ONUC from 1960 to 1964, making this country's military one of its most active members. For a time, Canadian brigadier general Jacques Dextraze was chief of staff for the UN mission and there were nearly always more Canadian officers at ONUC head-quarters than those of any other nationality.[10] Canadian troops within the UN force were also concentrated in militarily important logistical positions including chief operations officer and chief signals officer.[11] Describing the mission, military historians David Bercuson and Jack Granatstein wrote: "At headquarters, which operated in both French and English when sufficient bilingual offi-cers could be found, the Canadians handled everything from telephones to phones to dispatch riders. Indeed, to read Canadian messages to Ottawa, it often seemed as if Canadians were running everything."[12]

Canada's strategic role wasn't simply by chance. Ottawa pushed to have Canada's intelligence gathering signals detachments oversee UN intelligence and for colonel Jean Berthiaume to remain at UN headquarters to "maintain both Canadian and Western influence."[13]

A report from the Canadian Directorate of Military Intelligence noted that "Lumumba's immediate advisers… have referred to Lt. Col. Berthiaume as an 'imperialist tool.'"[14]

To bolster the power of ONUC, Ottawa joined Washington in channeling its development assistance to the Congo through the UN.[15] Ghanaian president Kwame Nkrumah complained that this was "applying a restriction to Congo which does not apply to any other African state."[16] Ottawa rejected Nkrumah's request to channel Congolese aid through independent African countries and to send 20 French-speaking members of the Canadian Armed Forces to help train Congolese cadets.[17] Either ignorant or aiming to offend, Prime Minister Diefenbaker denied the extremely impoverished country's request for assistance, arguing that "Canada, in a stage of great development, needed capital itself."[18] In response, Lumumba told a crowd he went to Canada "to seek bilateral aid in belief that it was a truly democratic land but had been disappointed to find that although honest, Canada was just another imperialist country."[19]

Diefenbaker and Lumumba had a public dispute on another occasion. When Canadian troops, mistaken for Belgian forces, were beaten by government soldiers, Diefenbaker drafted a letter of protest to Lumumba described as being "as strong as any employed by a Canadian head of government to a foreign leader."[20] To maximize the publicity, reporters were then called to Diefenbaker's office and shown the letter.[21]

Meanwhile Canada, unlike many ONUC participants, aggressively backed Hammarskjöld's controversial anti-Lumumba position. External Affairs Minister Green told the House of Commons: "The Canadian government will continue its firm support for the United Nations effort in the Congo and for Mr. Hammarskjöld, who in the face of the greatest difficulty has served the high principles and purposes of the charter with courage, determination and endless patience."[22]

Ottawa supported Hammarskjöld even as he sided with the Belgian-backed secessionists against the central government. On August 12, the UN secretary general travelled to Katanga and telegraphed secessionist leader Moïse Tshombe to discuss "deploying United Nations troops to Katanga."[23] Not even Belgium officially recognized Katanga's independence, provoking Issaka Soure to note, "[Hammarskjöld visit] sent a very bad signal by implicitly implying that the rebellious province could somehow be regarded as sovereign to the point that the UN chief administrator could deal with it directly."[24]

The UN head also worked to undermine Lumumba within the central government. When president Joseph Kasavubu dismissed Lumumba as prime minister—a move of debatable legality and opposed by the vast majority of the country's parliament—Hammarskjöld publicly endorsed the dismissal of a politician who a short time earlier had received the most votes in the country's election.[25]

Lumumba attempted to respond to his dismissal with a nationwide broadcast, but UN forces blocked him from accessing the main radio station.[26] ONUC also undermined Lumumba in other ways. Through their control of the airport, ONUC prevented his forces from flying into the capital from other parts of the country. When Lumumba turned to Moscow for assistance, the ONUC closed the airport to Soviet weapons and transportation equipment.[27] In addition, according to Bogle's *Hot Wars of the Cold Wars* "[the Secretary General's special representative Andrew] Cordier provided $1 million—money supplied to the United Nations by the US government—to [General Joseph] Mobutu in early September to pay off restive and hungry Congolese soldiers and keep them loyal to Kasavubu during his attempt to oust Lumumba as prime minister."[28]

To get a sense of Hammarskjöld's antipathy towards the Congolese leader, he privately told officials in Washington that Lumumba must be "broken" and only then would the Katanga problem "solve itself."[29] For his part, Cordier asserted that "Nkrumah is the Mussolini of Africa while Lumumba is its little Hitler."[30] Echoing this thinking, in a conversation with External Affairs Minister Green, Diefenbaker called Lumumba "a major threat to Western interests" and said that he was "coming around to the conclusion" that an independent Western-oriented Katanga offered "the best solution to the current crisis."[31]

In response to Hammarskjöld's efforts to undermine his leadership, Lumumba broke off relations with the secretary general.[32] He also called for the withdrawal of all non-African peacekeepers, which Hammarskjöld rejected as a threat to UN authority.[33] A number of ONUC nations ultimately took up Lumumba's protests. When the Congolese prime minister was overthrown and ONUC helped consolidate the coup, the United Arab Republic (Egypt and Syria), Guinea, Morocco, and Indonesia formally asked Hammarskjöld to withdraw all of their troops.

Canadian officials took a different position. They celebrated ONUC's role in Lumumba's overthrow. A week after Lumumba was pushed out, prominent Canadian diplomat Escott Reid, then ambassador to Germany, noted in an internal letter, "already the United Nations has demonstrated in the Congo that it can in Africa act as the executive agent of the free world."[34]

The "free world" was complicit in the murder of one of Africa's most important independence leaders. In fact, the top Canadian in ONUC directly enabled his killing.

After Lumumba escaped house arrest and fled Léopoldville for his power base in the eastern Orientale province, colonel Jean Berthiaume assisted Lumumba's political enemies by helping recapture him. The UN chief of staff, who was kept in place by Ottawa, tracked the deposed prime minister and informed Joseph Mobutu of Lumumba's whereabouts. Three decades later Berthiaume told an interviewer:

> I called Mobutu. I said, Colonel, you have a problem, you were trying to retrieve your prisoner, Mr. Lumumba. I

know where he is, and I know where he will be tomor-
row. He said, what do I do? It's simple, Colonel, with
the help of the UN you have just created the core of
your para commandos—we have just trained 30 of these
guys—highly selected Moroccans trained as paratroopers. They all jumped—no one refused. To be on the safe
side, I put our [Canadian] captain, Mario Coté, in the
plane, to make sure there was no underhandedness. In
any case, it's simple, you take a Dakota [plane], send
your paratroopers and arrest Lumumba in that small
village—there is a runway and all that is needed. That's
all you'll need to do, Colonel. He arrested him, like that,
and I never regretted it.[35]

Ghanaian peacekeepers near where Lumumba was
captured took quite a different attitude towards the
elected prime minister's safety. After Mobutu's forces
captured Lumumba, they requested permission to
intervene and place Lumumba under UN protection.[36]
Unfortunately, their request was denied by the secretary
general. Not long thereafter Lumumba was beaten, executed by firing squad, and his body dissolved in acid.

The Diefenbaker government gave its approval of
Lumumba's capture and his treatment by Mobutu's
forces. After receiving news of the Congolese leader's arrest, Green told the House of Commons that
Lumumba should "be brought to a fair and speedy
trial in accordance with the guarantees which are nor-
mally given to accused persons." When he was asked
if Ottawa protested Lumumba's beating in custody,
Green's reply was shockingly callous. "No," he said,
"there has been no protest launched. It would keep us

very busy if we were to protest all the beatings which take place in the Congo."[37]

At the time that Green made this statement, Lumumba had already been murdered. When news of Lumumba's death reached Diefenbaker, he reportedly did not express his revulsion. Instead, he "speculated on the likelihood that Lumumba's left-leaning successor [and former deputy prime minister], Antoine Gizenga, would strengthen his position in the Congo."

He did not have to worry about Gizenga for long. After conspiring to eliminate Lumumba, the UN helped imprison Gizenga too. Upon Lumumba's death, Gizenga had established a government in Orientale province that was recognized by 20 African and Asian countries, but in 1962 his administration was crushed by the UN and Congolese army.

With the country's progressive forces weakened by Lumumba's death and Gizenga's imprisonment, Katanga's secessionists were no longer useful to the Western powers, so the UN proceeded to violently suppress the same movement they tacitly supported while Lumumba was in power. At least 300 UN soldiers died fighting to maintain the Congo's territorial integrity.

Foreign resource companies and Western geopolitical interests were the main beneficiaries of UN operations in the Congo. The leading Congolese beneficiary of the UN mission was Joseph Mobutu who went on to run the country for over three decades.

Mobutu developed close ties to Canadian political and military officials. In a 1992 interview Canadian diplomat Michel Gauvin said that "during my time in Léopoldville as Chargé d'Affaires [from 1961 to 1963] I got to know Mobutu very well, I was one of the only whites invited to the baptism of one of his girls."[38] In *In the Eye of the Storm: A History of Canadian Peacekeeping*, Fred Gaffen explains·

> Mobutu learned to trust the Canadian officers. This trust was of inestimable value in arranging ceasefires between Congolese and UN forces, negotiating the release of prisoners as well as liaising between UN and Congolese authorities. Mobutu, who became president of the Democratic Republic of Zaire, visited Canada in May of 1964. At that time, he thanked those Canadian officers who had contributed so much to the maintenance of the unity of the country.[39]

Kwame Nkrumah, who Canada would help overthrow a few years later, described the UN's complicity in Lumumba's murder:

> Somewhere in Katanga in the Congo ... three of our brother freedom fighters have been done to death. ... about their end many things are uncertain, but one fact is crystal clear. They have been killed because the United Nations whom Patrice Lumumba himself as Prime Minister had invited to the Congo to preserve law and order, not only failed to maintain that law and order, but also denied to the lawful government of the Congo all other means of self-protection. History records many occasions when rulers of states have been assassinated. The murder of Patrice Lumumba and of his two colleagues, however, is unique in that it is the first time in history that the legal ruler of a country has been done to death with the open connivance of a world

organization in whom that ruler put his trust ... instead of preserving law and order, the United Nations declared itself neutral between law and disorder and refused to lend any assistance whatsoever to the legal government in suppressing the mutineers who had set themselves up in power in Katanga and South Kasai. When, in order to move its troops against the rebels, the government of the Congo obtained some civilian aircraft and civilian motor vehicles from the Soviet Union, the colonialist powers at the United Nations raised a howl of rage while, at the same time maintaining a discreet silence over the buildup of Belgian arms and actual Belgian military forces in the service of the rebels ... when Lumumba [after Kasavubu's coup] wished to broadcast to the people explaining what happened, the United Nations in the so-called interest of law and order prevented him by force from speaking. They did not, however, use the same force to prevent the mutineers of the Congolese army from seizing power in Leopoldville and installing a completely illegal government ... the United Nations sat by while the so-called Katanga government, which is entirely Belgian controlled, imported aircraft and arms from Belgium and other countries, such as [apartheid] South Africa, which have a vested interest in the suppression of African freedom. The United Nations connived at the setting up, in fact of an independent Katanga state, though this is contrary to the Security Council's own resolutions. Finally, the United Nations, which could exert its authority to prevent Patrice Lumumba from broadcasting, was, so it pleaded, quite unable to prevent his arrest by mutineers or his transfer, through the use of airfields under United Nations control, into the hands of the Belgian-dominated government of Katanga.[40]

The UN mission to the Congo, in which Canada participated actively, facilitated a major injustice and crime against the Congolese people.

THE DOMINICAN REPUBLIC, 1963

In late 1962, the leftist Juan Bosch won the Dominican Republic's first clean election with 59% of the vote. At first backed by the US government as a reformer who could mediate the excesses of the increasingly embarrassing Rafael Trujillo dictatorship, Bosch proved to be more than the toothless politician Washington desired. After three decades of Trujillo family rule, Bosch encouraged civil society by training co-operative, union, and peasant leaders. The Dominican president also moved to break up some of the country's large plantations and pushed constitutional changes that expanded the rights of labour, women, and children. These moves were not welcomed by the right-wing church establishment or economic elite that had built up tremendous wealth under Trujillo. Nor was Washington happy, which saw "another Cuba" in Bosch's mild but important reforms.

After seven months in office, Bosch was exiled in a military coup backed by industrialists, large land-owners, and the church. With Washington's support, the elected government was replaced by a three-man military junta. US Senator J. W. Fulbright stated that "the United States turned its back on social revolution in Santo Domingo and associated itself with a corrupt and reactionary military oligarchy."[1] Bosch himself later wrote that "the most influential strata of the population [the upper and middle classes] joined with political leaders...in a conspiracy to defeat the democratic government."[2]

Growing dissatisfaction with the coup regime spurred a military counter-rebellion led by "constitutionalist" forces demanding Bosch be restored to office. After the coup regime was successfully removed from power, the US intervened. At the end of April 1965, the Lyndon B. Johnson administration dispatched more than 20,000 US troops to the Dominican Republic, almost half the number of US soldiers then in Vietnam.[3] Johnson blamed Cuban-trained communist operatives for the uprising against the unelected military regime. On May 2, 1965, the President claimed that "Communist leaders, many of them trained in Cuba, seeing a chance to increase disorder, to gain a foothold, joined the revolution. They took increasing control. And what began as a popular democratic revolution ... very shortly moved and was taken over and really seized and placed into the hands of a band of Communist conspirators."[4] Therefore, he argued, the US had to invade to protect "progress, democracy ... social justice [and] the principles of the inter-American system."[5]

Despite touting the invasion as a necessary measure to protect the "inter-American system," Johnson did not seem bothered by the fact that the military intervention was a violation of the Organization of American States (OAS) charter. The US administration had failed to inform Latin American member states of the invasion beforehand, an "open contravention of articles 15 and 17 of the OAS charter."[6]

In response to the invasion, prime minister Lester B. Pearson told Parliament: "the United States government has intervened in the Dominican Republic for the protection of its own citizens and those of other countries."[7] When asked whether the "United States has the right to violate the sovereign rights of the Dominican Republic by the landing of marines," Pearson said: "I think it is well known in international law—indeed it is accepted in the Organization of American States— that a government has the responsibility for protecting its own people in situations of insurrection and disturbance when those citizens are in danger and when the forces of law and order seem to have temporarily disappeared."[8] Secretary of state for external affairs, Paul Martin Sr., also jumped to the defense of the Johnson administration, stating: "It is easy to criticize countries which bear the brunt of responsibility when dangerous situations develop. Such criticism might best be directed at the imperfections of our international arrangements."[9]

The government continued to defend US actions even after it was clear Washington was not simply protecting US civilians. Three weeks after the US deployed its troops, an NDP MP referred to the "invasion of this Republic by the United States," prompting External Affairs Minister Martin to complain about this "extravagant characterization" of "the American interest in Latin America and the Dominican Republic."[10]

Ottawa rejected a request by "constitutionalist" general, Francisco Caamaño, appointed President until Bosch could return, for diplomatic recognition. In explaining his decision, Pearson told Parliament "there are indeed communists in the directing group who are controlling that particular ... group seeking recognition."[11]

While a Canadian warship in the Caribbean was sent "to stand by in case it is required," a few Latin American countries sent troops to participate in an Organization of American States mission designed to relieve US troops from the country.[12] On May 28 Pearson told the House: "I am sure we would all wish to see this [OAS] force carry out successfully its functions of bringing peace and stability to the Dominican Republic."[13]

A year after invading, the US set up "demonstration elections" won by a former Trujillo official, Joaquin Balaguer. The Pearson government supported Balaguer with one of its first bilateral grants to a Latin American country. Canada gave $298,000 in food aid to the Dominican Republic in 1966 as part of the "mop-up in the wake of the 1965 military invasion of that country."[14] After Balaguer was entrenched as head of state, Pearson instructed Canadian officials not to publicly criticize US policy in the Dominican Republic.[15]

Ottawa supported the US invasion partly out of concern for Canadian investments in the country, including mining giant Falconbridge, which cooperated with Trujillo during the latter years of his dictatorship. Following Bosch's 1963 removal by the military, Paul Martin Sr. told Parliament, "We have ... been in touch by telephone with the Falconbridge Nickel plant ... and we are told that all is well in that quarter."[16] Later he said that "the embassy is also investigating reports that the main branch of the Royal Bank of Canada has been looted."[17] Concern for Canadian corporate assets was driven by the size of the investments. At this time Canadian banking interests held nearly 70% of the Dominican Republic's foreign-owned banking assets.[18] Falconbridge's interests in the Dominican Republic were not insignificant either and the US intervention was good for business.

The year after the invasion, Falconbridge quadrupled the size of its experimental pilot plant in the country. By the 1970s, John Harbron of the *Financial Times* reported that Ian Keith, the CEO of Falcondo, Falconbridge's Dominican operations, "has become an intimate part of Dominican public life, as much as the emerging elite of presidents and managers of rejuvenating Dominican public and private companies who are absorbing some of Falcondo's way of doing things."[19] By 1972, this viciously anti-union employer controlled the single largest foreign investment in the country, and earned the ardent support of the new US-backed dictator Joaquin Balaguer.

In 1971, Balaguer personally presented Falconbridge CEO Marsh Cooper with the Order of Merit of Duarte, Sánchez, and Mella, the highest honour bestowed by the government for distinguished services to the

Dominican Republic. He pointed to the Canadian company's presence on the island as an indication that his government was a legitimate and stable actor following the period of instability, telling the *Wall Street Journal*, "Among the sure signs of the climate of security and confidence the Dominican Republic offers foreign investors [is] the installation of the enormous metallurgical plant by the Falconbridge Co. of Canada."[20]

While some corporations benefitted, other Canadians objected to the government's moves. *Our Place in the Sun* explains: "the PCM [progressive church movement] excoriated the government of Lester B. Pearson for having supported the US invasion of the Dominican Republic."[21]

BRAZIL, 1964

In 1964, Brazil's military overthrew the country's elected government headed by left-leaning president João Goulart. Having assumed power following the resignation of President Jânio Quadros in August 1961, Goulart sought to lift Brazil from political and socioeconomic crisis by implementing his *Reformas de Base* (Basic Reforms) program, which included efforts to combat adult illiteracy, increase taxes on the profits of foreign-based companies, and a number of redistributive measures including land reform. Goulart also wanted to expand suffrage by giving illiterate people and low-ranking military officers the right to vote. He proposed putting 15% of the national income into education. To pay for this, the government planned to introduce a proportional income tax and greater controls on the profit transfers of multinational corporations.

Additionally, Goulart enacted an independent foreign policy. He affirmed Cuba's right to self-determination while entertaining cordial relations with the Soviet Union and China. Goulart wanted Washington to be more flexible regarding the terms of its assistance and criticized the Kennedy administration's Alliance for Progress, a regional development program aimed at promoting anti-communism in recipient nations.

The Kennedy administration was angered at what it considered "an open declaration of war on the Alliance for Progress."[1]

When Goulart threatened to increase Brazil's economic cooperation with the Soviet Union, US ambassador Lincoln Gordon claimed he was threatening to create "a second Yugoslavia at best and a second Cuba at worst." Gordon said Goulart's threat "impressed me once again with Goulart's basic incapacity to be (the) president (of a) large country."[2] In the event that Goulart proceeded with his *Reformas de Base* model of development, the ambassador stated that "we must consider all possible means (for) promoting (a) change in regime."[3]

Washington, Ottawa, and leading segments of Brazil's business community opposed Goulart's foreign policy and *Reformas de Base*. Two and a half years into his presidency the Brazilian military and conservative political elements organized his ouster.

When the coup came in April 1964, Washington backed it fully. At one point, President Lyndon Johnson urged ambassador Gordon to take "every step that we can" to support Goulart's removal. In a declassified cable between Gordon and Washington, the ambassador in Brasília acknowledged US involvement in "covert support for pro-democracy street rallies ... and encouragement [of] democratic and anti-communist sentiment in Congress, armed forces, friendly labor and student groups, church, and business."[4]

Ottawa failed to publicly condemn the ouster of Goulart. "The Canadian reaction to the military coup of 1964 was careful, polite and allied with American rhetoric," notes Barbosa in *Brazil and Canada in the Americas*.[5]

As important as following Washington's lead, the Lester B. Pearson government's tacit support for the coup was also driven by Canadian corporate interests. The Toronto-based firm Brascan (formerly Brazilian Traction) was active in Brazil at the time. Commonly known as "the Canadian octopus" because its tentacles reached into so many areas of Brazil's economy, Brascan was among the largest companies in Latin America at the time. A study of the firm noted, "[Brazilian Traction's vice-president Antonio] Gallotti doesn't hide his participation in the moves and operations that led to the coup d'état against Goulart in 1964."[6] Just prior to the coup, Brazilian Traction president Grant Glassco remarked, "more and more, the various agencies of the government were infiltrated by extremists, many of whom were Communist inspired and directed."[7] After Goulart was overthrown, Glassco stated "the new government of Brazil is ... made up of men of proven competence and integrity. The President, Humberto Castelo Branco, commands the respect of the entire nation."[8]

Putting a stop to the Goulart government, which made it more difficult for companies to export profits, was good business.[9] After the 1964 coup, the *Financial Post* noted "the price of Brazilian Traction common shares almost doubled overnight with the change of government from an April 1 low of $1.95 to an April 3 high of

$3.06."[10] Between 1965 and 1974, Brascan drained Brazil of $342 million ($2 billion today).[11] When Brascan's Canadian president, Robert Winters, was asked why the company's profits grew so rapidly in the late 1960s his response was simple: "The Revolution."[12]

Before he took charge of Brascan, Winters was Canada's trade minister. Similarly, Jack Nicholson, a Brazilian Traction chief executive in Brazil in the 1950s, held a number of cabinet positions in the Pearson government.[13] Long-time Liberal civil servant, Mitchell Sharp, went from deputy minister in the Department of Trade and Commerce to vice-president of Brascan. A year before the coup, Pearson appointed him finance minister.

The coup against Goulart brought to power a military dictatorship that ruled Brazil for over two decades. The regime served as a counter-revolutionary bastion for neighbouring right-wing dictatorships, and it received the support of Washington, Ottawa, and their allies including Pinochet's Chile and Israel.

INDONESIA, 1965

In a coordinated campaign to prevent the spread of leftism in Asia, Western countries including the US, Britain, and Canada supported the overthrow of Indonesia's independence leader Sukarno in 1965 and the subsequent murder of half a million suspected supporters.

Initially, Canada backed Dutch colonialism during the Indonesian war of independence. However, the Canadian position took a turn in 1948 when Sukarno appeared to be a reliably pro-Western and anti-communist leader. By the early 1960s, Canada's attitude changed. Sukarno's willingness to recognize the legitimacy of the Indonesian Communist Party (PKI) and other endogenous left-wing and progressive movements irked the North American and the European powers, as did his tendency to publicly criticize Western imperialism in Asia and his leading role in the anti-colonial Non-Aligned Movement.

In a bid to maintain its influence in East Asia, in mid-1961 London pushed to merge its colonies of North Borneo, Sarawak, and Singapore with Malaya (technically independent from England since 1957) to create Malaysia. Indonesia objected to what it saw as a subservient Malaysian government's willingness to extend colonial authority on its border. Conflict between Indonesia and Malaysia escalated into a low-level war.

Ottawa sided with the Malaysian leader Tunku. During a visit to Ottawa by Tunku, prime minister Lester B. Pearson said "under his leadership the peoples of Malaysia have been brought closer together in freedom, democracy and greater human welfare" despite Indonesian "pressure dedicated to their destruction."[1] In *Fire and the Full Moon*, David Webster notes, "Ottawa avoided direct military involvement but was clearly a partisan and on the Malaysian side."[2] In the midst of the conflict, Canada cut a small disbursement of food aid to Indonesia while releasing $4 million ($28 million today) in military aid to Malaysia.[3] In response, Indonesian President Sukarno added Canada to his list of "imperialists with white skins," which included the US, New Zealand, Australia, and Britain.[4] A nationalist Indonesian newspaper, *Suluh*, said Ottawa should "go to hell."[5]

An External Affairs assessment of Indonesian foreign policy during this period concluded that Sukarno wanted "an endless succession of foreign adventures" to satisfy his "personal and national megalomania."[6] Canada's ambassador in Jakarta further explained: "He [Sukarno] wants revolutionary change in the balance of economic power between the developed and less developed nations ... We believe that under Sukarno Indonesia is already a lost cause as far as the free world is concerned."[7]

Sukarno's aggressive opposition to British policy in Malaysia hastened a slow-moving US-backed military takeover, which included the eventual slaughter of 500,000 Indonesian "communists." Enabled by external and internal dynamics, Major General Suharto oversaw a wave of terror in late 1965 that left hundreds of thousands of landless peasants and Communist Party members dead.[8] Commander of the Army Strategic Reserve, Suharto then overthrew democratically elected Sukarno. In the lead-up to this bloody military coup, the US government authorized a covert program in late 1964 to assist the "good men in the government, armed services and the private sector" who might topple Sukarno if Washington supported their efforts.[9] Washington also worked to paint the PKI as an agent of China and enemy of Indonesian nationalism.

Pearson's government backed the Indonesian general's repressive political machinations. Even though he was aware of Suharto's killing, in early 1966 Canada's ambassador in Jakarta called this mass murderer "a moderate, sensible and progressive leader."[10] An External Affairs memorandum explained: "Changes in the political orientation of Indonesia have already had a profound effect on the prospects for stability in South East Asia. It is patently in our interests that the new [Suharto] regime be able to consolidate its internal position and to pursue external policies it appears prepared to follow. These are policies which promise to make the situation much easier not only for the smaller countries of the area but also for Australia, New Zealand, the UK and the USA."[11]

One of the most important actions implemented by the Suharto government following the coup was the "Stabilization Plan." The Stabilization Plan was a boon to foreign investors, including companies headquartered in Canada. It established "tax holidays, provisions for unrestricted repatriation of profits, exemptions from import duties, and cutbacks in government participation in the economy."[12] Canadian companies Bata Shoes and International Nickel Company (INCO) benefitted.[13]

To aid Suharto, Ottawa selected Indonesia as the main Asian country outside of the Commonwealth to receive Canadian aid.[14] *Rain Dancing* explains: "The domestic political stability achieved by Suharto after the ouster of Sukarno in 1966, together with a pronounced tilt in foreign policy towards the West, made Indonesia an attractive target in the eyes of [Canadian] policymakers."[15] Ottawa preferred Suharto's Western-trained technocrats to Sukarno's anti-colonial nationalism.[16] "Only with the removal of Sukarno from power," notes Webster, "would the Government of Canada smile on Indonesia again."[17]

GHANA, 1966

During a visit to Ghana in 2012 Canadian governor general Michaëlle Jean laid a wreath on the tomb of former president Kwame Nkrumah. But, in commemorating this leading pan-Africanist, she failed to acknowledge the substantial role her country played in his downfall. In February 1966 Ghana's Canadian-trained army overthrew Nkrumah, a leader dubbed "Man of the Millennium" in a 2000 poll by BBC listeners in Africa.

Washington, together with London, backed the coup. Lester Pearson's government also gave its blessing to Nkrumah's ouster and his replacement by a military-led government. In *The Deceptive Ash: Bilingualism and Canadian Policy in Africa: 1957-1971*, John P. Schlegel writes: "the Western orientation and the more liberal approach of the new military government was welcomed by Canada."[1]

The coup d'état was a largely CIA-orchestrated reaction against Nkrumah's deepening alliances with the Soviet Union and Maoist China, as well as his state's commitment to transitioning Africa away from an outward-oriented economic model toward an inward-facing national development plan. Nkrumah also espoused pan-Africanist ideology, or the belief that he and his allies were "not fighting for African liberation only, we are fighting also for the political unification of Africa, for without unity there can be no future for the African People."

In Nkrumah's political writing, most notably 1965's *Neo-Colonialism*, the independence leader researched the mechanisms by which Western states and transnational companies exploited Africa's material wealth. He illustrated how private investment from US companies had increased massively after the granting of formal independence. So had the profits they drew from the continent. Nkrumah pointed out that US power was gradually overtaking European supremacy in Africa, and that this power was not sustained through direct political control, but through "neocolonial" economic control.

As the president, Nkrumah took an active role in supporting anti-colonial struggles throughout Africa, including in the Western-backed apartheid regimes of Southern Africa. Outside the continent Nkrumah joined India's Jawaharlal Nehru, Indonesia's Ahmed Sukarno, and Yugoslavia's Josip Broz Tito in championing Cold War non-alignment. He participated in many important "Third World" conferences in Africa and abroad, including the 1955 Bandung Conference, which Indonesian president Sukarno described as "the first intercontinental conference of coloured peoples."

The day Nkrumah was overthrown, the Canadian prime minister was asked in the House of Commons his opinion about this development. Pearson said nothing of substance on the matter. The next day external affairs minister Paul Martin Sr. responded to questions about Canada's military training in Ghana, saying there was no change in instructions. In response to an MP's question about recognizing the military government, Martin said: "In many cases recognition is accorded automatically. In respective cases such as that which occurred in Ghana yesterday, the practice is developing of carrying on with the government which has taken over, but according no formal act until some interval has elapsed. We shall carry on with the present arrangement for Ghana. Whether there will be any formal act will depend on information which is not now before us."[2]

While Martin and Pearson were measured in public, the Canadian high commissioner in Accra, C.E. McGaughey, was not. In an internal memo to External Affairs just after Nkrumah was overthrown, McGaughey wrote that "a wonderful thing has happened for the West in Ghana and Canada has played a worthy part." Referring to the coup, the high commissioner added that "all here welcome this development except party functionaries and communist diplomatic missions." He then applauded the Ghanaian military for having "thrown the Russian and Chinese rascals out."[3]

Less than two weeks after the coup, the Pearson government informed the military junta that Canada intended to carry on normal relations.[4] In the immediate aftermath of Nkrumah's overthrow, Canada sent $1.82 million ($15 million today) worth of flour to

Ghana and offered the military regime a hundred CUSO volunteers.[5] For its part, the International Monetary Fund (IMF), which had previously severed financial assistance to Nkrumah's government, engaged immediately after the coup by restructuring Ghana's debt. Canada's contribution was an outright gift. During the three years between 1966 and 1969, the National Liberation Council military regime received as much Canadian aid as during Nkrumah's ten years in office with $22 million in grants and loans. Ottawa was the fourth major donor after the US, UK and UN.[6]

Two months after Nkrumah's ouster the Canadian high commissioner in Ghana wrote to Montréal-based De Havilland Aircraft with a request to secure parts for Ghana's Air Force. Worried Nkrumah might attempt a counter coup, the Air Force sought parts for non-operational aircraft in the event it needed to deploy its forces.[7]

Six months after overthrowing Nkrumah, the country's new leader, General Joseph Ankrah, made an official visit to Ottawa as part of a trip that also took him through London and Washington.[8]

More important than the diplomatic and economic support for Nkrumah's ouster, Canada provided military training. Schlegel described the military government as a "product of this military training program."[9] A Canadian major who was a training advisor to the commander of a Ghanaian infantry brigade discovered preparations for the coup the day before its execution. Bob Edwards said nothing.[10] After Nkrumah's removal the Canadian high commissioner boasted about the effectiveness of Canada's Junior Staff Officer's training program at the Ghanaian Defence College. Writing to the Canadian under secretary of external affairs, McGaughey noted that "all the chief participants of the coup were graduates of this course."[11]

After independence Ghana's army remained British dominated. The colonial era British generals were still in place and the majority of Ghana's officers continued to be trained in Britain. In response to a number of embarrassing incidents, Nkrumah released the British commanders in September 1961. It was at this point that Canada began training Ghana's military.

While Canadians organized and oversaw the Junior Staff Officers course, a number of Canadians took up top positions in the Ghanaian Ministry of Defence. In the words of Canada's military attaché to Ghana, Colonel Desmond Deane-Freeman, the Canadians in these positions imparted "our way of thinking."[12] Celebrating the influence of "our way of thinking," in 1965 High Commissioner McGaughey wrote the under secretary of external affairs: "Since independence, it [Ghana's military] has changed in outlook, perhaps less than any other institution. It is still equipped with Western arms and although essentially non-political, is Western oriented."[13]

Not everyone was happy with the military's attitude or Canada's role therein. A year after Nkrumah's ouster, McGaughey wrote Ottawa: "For some African and Asian diplomats stationed in Accra, I gather that there is a tendency to identify our aid policies particularly where military assistance is concerned with the aims of American and British policies. American and British objectives are unfortunately not regarded by such observers as being above criticism or suspicion."[14] Thomas Howell and Jeffrey Rajasooria echo the high commissioner's assessment in their book *Ghana and Nkrumah*: "Members of the ruling CPP tended to identify Canadian aid policies, especially in defence areas, with the aims of the U.S. and Britain. Opponents of the Canadian military program went so far as to create a countervailing force in the form of the Soviet equipped, pro-communist President's Own Guard Regiment [POGR]. The coup on 24 February 1966 which ousted Kwame Nkrumah and the CPP was partially rooted in this divergence of military loyalty."[15]

The POGR became a "direct rival" to the Canadian-trained army, notes Christopher Kilford in *The Other Cold War: Canada's Military Assistance to the Developing World, 1945-1975*.[16] Even once Canadian officials in Ottawa "well understood" Canada's significant role in the internal military battle developing in Ghana, writes Kilford, "there was never any serious discussion around withdrawing the Canadian training team."[17]

As the 1960s wore on, Nkrumah's government became increasingly critical of London and Washington's support for the white minority in southern Africa. Ottawa had little sympathy for Nkrumah's pan-African ideals and so it made little sense to continue training the Ghanaian Army if it was, in Kilford's words, to "be used to further Nkrumah's political aims." Kilford continued his thought, stating "that is unless the Canadian government believed that in time a well-trained, professional Ghana Army might soon remove Nkrumah."[18]

The post-Nkrumah military government destroyed the president's socialist project and massively liberalized the country's economy. It also reduced the country's support for the liberation of other African territories.[19] After his overthrow in 1966, Nkrumah noted that the Western-supported military government "went on to close down the training camps for freedom fighters in Ghana…I [had] set up the training camps in Ghana with the co-operation of freedom fighters from all over Africa. Their purpose was to provide training for those intending to win freedom for Africans in Rhodesia, Angola, Mozambique, South Africa, so-called Portuguese Guinea, and the Cape Verde Islands, and in South West Africa."[20]

GREECE, 1967

In April 1967, Canada tacitly endorsed a military coup in Greece, a fellow member of NATO. Shortly before an election expected to bring Andreas Papandreou of the social democratic Centre Union to power, right-wing colonels seized power. The new junta claimed they protected Greece from a "communist coup" and promised national "regeneration" along the lines of "Helleno-Christian" traditions.[1]

The US actively supported the coup. In the leadup to the scheduled election, US ambassador Phillips Talbot stated, "the Greek nation would never be delivered to the communists or to Andreas Papandreou. It would be saved for real democracy."[2] When the junta imprisoned Papandreou after the coup, CIA liaison Gust Avrakotos officially urged his release but quietly told the colonels to "shoot the motherfucker."[3] Papandreou was eventually expelled from the country.

Canada did not condemn the coup. As Christopher Grafos writes, "the Canadian government remained neutral on the subject and insisted that it cannot get involved in another country's internal affairs."[4] This was the official NATO position, as Western leaders believed the new military rulers to be "ardent NATOists."[5] Responding to criticism that Canada was supporting fascist NATO governments in Greece and

Portugal, secretary of state for external affairs Mitchell Sharp stated that "to offer specific, pointed criticism of these allies would do little to enhance private overtures to these governments."[6]

A year after the coup Papandreou gave a speech at Toronto's Varsity Stadium in which he asserted that "all countries supporting the junta were his enemies," implying that Canada was collaborating with his foe.[7] At the same time, the Committee for the Restoration of Democracy in Greece (CRDG) sent multiple letters to members of the Pierre Trudeau government asking them to reconsider their quietly pro-junta position. In a letter to external affairs minister Paul Martin Sr., the Committee stated, "we are asking the Canadian Government not to recognize the military dictatorship in Greece."[8]

Alongside Papandreou, many Greek exiles ended up in Canada following the coup. Many of them organized anti-dictatorship action and tried to pressure the Canadian government to rescind its support for the junta, including by suspending military aid.

The RCMP monitored anti-junta exile groups operating in Canada, particularly communist groups. They infiltrated political meetings, collected information from right-wing Greeks who supported the junta, and occasionally visited the homes of pro-democracy organizers to question them.[9] Katherine Pendakis, who interviewed many politically active Greeks in Canada during the junta years, found that many organized pro-democracy protests under "inhospitable conditions created by

Canada's anticommunist political culture [and] RCMP surveillance."[10] One RCMP file focused on the fact that the CRDG distributed a leaflet that mentioned an Amnesty International report on the treatment of political prisoners under the junta.[11]

The RCMP were not the only ones monitoring pro-democracy activities among Greeks in Canada. The Greek Embassy spied on CRDG and other leftists, sometimes employing right-wing Greeks to collect information. The embassy lobbied Ottawa not to legitimize Papandreou's anti-dictatorship stance by recognizing his organization. When Papandreou claimed his organization received "official recognition" from Canada, the junta responded with incredulity, demanding Ottawa explain itself. Canada's European Division expressed sympathy with the junta, writing: "The [Greek] Ambassador's annoyance is easy to understand in view of the organization's claim of 'official recognition' and statement that contributions are deductible for tax purposes. He doubtless considers (perhaps correctly) that the Fund has been created as a money-making agency for Papandreou's various activities including the 'Pan-Hellenic Liberation Front.'"[12]

Sharp's under-secretary A.E. Ritchie also sided with the junta: "You will appreciate that the statement by the organization that it is 'officially recognized by the Canadian Government' causes us some embarrassment in view of the fact that its chairman, Andreas Papandreou is well known for his political activity in Canada against the Greek Government …

Mr. Papandreou is on record as having called for the violent overthrow of the present Greek Government. From private sources, we understand that he has been collecting money for this purpose."[13]

While endorsing Western interventions in left-leaning countries like the Congo, Dominican Republic, Brazil, and Ghana, Ottawa argued that supporting anti-fascist forces in Greece amounted to interference in a friendly country. "Whatever one may think of this objective," Sharp wrote about Papandreou's organization, "it is clear that, if the Canadian government endorsed it, it would be intervening in the domestic affairs of a friendly and allied country. Any support which might imply official endorsement of the Panhellenic Liberation Movement could, therefore, have serious repercussions."[14]

For whatever reason, Ottawa apparently did not consider the junta's spying in Canada to be "intervening in the domestic affairs of a friendly and allied country."

It wasn't until 1973, one year before the junta's collapse, that the Canadian government voiced its official disapproval of political developments in Greece, noting "regret" over the colonels' "failure to normalise the Greek political situation."[15] Until that point, criticism of Greece's fascist turn was considered unwarranted interference in the affairs of a NATO ally.

UGANDA, 1971

In 1971, Uganda's post-independence leader Milton Obote was overthrown by general Idi Amin with the aid of Britain, Israel, and the US. Ottawa passively supported the putsch. Obote admired Ghanian independence leader Kwame Nkrumah, who was overthrown in 1966 with Canadian assistance, and was a firm critic of US policy in Africa and Southeast Asia. Irving Gershenberg described Obote as "a man whose personal dedication to socialism was widely accepted in Africa."[1] His successor, Amin, was a military dictator whose rule aligned with Western interests on the continent until he later proved too erratic.

Obote's government was the first in East Africa to join the Soviet Union in condemning US policy in Vietnam, decrying "the aggression of American imperialism against the peoples of Vietnam and the whole of Indo-China."[2] Obote visited China and opposed Western support for the apartheid governments in Southern Africa. He referred to Moïse Tshombe, the anti-Lumumba leader in the Congo, as "the imperialist stooge."[3] These moves alienated him from Western governments and domestic conservative opponents alike. Ali Mazrui explains:

> Renewed fears that Obote might be taking the country towards socialism, and endangering certain traditional

institutions in Uganda, were activated. Obote's tour of Communist countries … seemed to confirm some of these apprehensions. Possibilities of mutual sympathies between Ugandan conservatives and opponents of Obote, on the one hand, and Western Embassies and other Western interests on the other, were emerging. Domestic enemies of Obote were beginning to calculate on the likelihood of getting external Western support should there be a confrontation between themselves and Obote at home.[4]

Obote feared he would face Nkrumah's fate: a military coup carried out by Western-trained officers. To pre-empt this possibility, he suspended the constitution in 1966 and took over executive power.

Following the 1966 coup against Nkrumah, Obote turned into the new target in the war on Pan-Africanism and African socialism. Idi Amin became the West's representative in that war. Popular UK historian Mark Curtis explains: "Britain consciously supported and connived in the rise of Idi Amin because of long-standing British interests to get rid of governments like that of Obote" whose economic policies threatened its corporate interests.[5] A Foreign Office memo noted that Obote's nationalizations, which also included Canada's Bata Shoes and Falconbridge, had "serious implications for British business in Uganda and Africa generally … other countries will be tempted to try and get away with similar measures with more damaging consequences for British investment and trade."[6]

In 1968, Obote increased the country's copper export tax and then moved to gain majority control of Falconbridge's massive Kilembe copper-cobalt mine in the western part of the country. This was part of a leftward turn "aimed at setting Uganda upon a socialist path of social, political, and economic development."[7] In *Falconbridge: Portrait of a Canadian Mining Multinational,* John Deverell explains: "Although Kilembe Copper was both profitable and socially important in the Ugandan economy, this did not prevent the Falconbridge group from withdrawing capital as rapidly as possible just before president Obote forced it to sell Uganda a controlling interest in 1970. The implication was that its management team would be withdrawn entirely if the government did not restore Falconbridge's majority ownership. Dislocation in the lives of Ugandan people was a price the company seemed willing to pay in this tug-of-war over the profits from Uganda's resources."[8]

In January 1971, elements of the military led by Amin overthrew the government. Gershenberg, who was holed up in the Makerere University at the time, described hearing "the staccato of rifle, machine gun, and anti-tank fire" in the streets of Kampala, followed by a warrant officer explaining over Radio Uganda that the military had overthrown Obote because of eighteen grievances that related to his economic ideology and policies.[9] Upon taking office, General Amin returned control of the Kilembe mine to Falconbridge (this was maintained for several years, after which Amin returned the mine to his government).

Little has been published about Ottawa's position on Amin's rise to power. The available documentation suggests Ottawa quietly supported the putsch. On three occasions during the early days of the coup (between January 26 and February 3, 1971), the Pierre Trudeau government responded to inquiries from opposition MPs about developments in Uganda and whether Canada would grant diplomatic recognition to the new regime. Within a week of Obote's ouster, both external affairs minister Mitchell Sharp and Prime Minister Trudeau passed up these opportunities to denounce Amin's usurpation of power. They remained silent as Amin suspended various provisions of the Ugandan Constitution and declared himself president, commander in chief of the armed forces, Army chief of staff and chief of air staff. They failed to condemn a leader, now infamous, for plunging the nation into a torrent of violence.

In *African Pearls and Poisons: Idi Amin's Uganda; Kenya; Zaire's Pygmies,* Alberta bureaucrat Leo Louis Jacques describes a conversation he had with the Canadian International Development Agency (CIDA) liaison officer in Uganda who facilitated his 1971-73 appointment to the Uganda College of Commerce. Asked whether the change in government would affect his CIDA-funded position, the aid agency's liaison officer in Uganda, Catrina Porter, answered Jacques thusly: "'Yes, there was a coup on January 25th, 1971 and it was a move that promises to be an improvement. The new administration favours Democracy and Western Civilization's Democracy, while the former one favoured the Communists.' I [Jacques] said,

'I understand the present government is being run by the Ugandan army under the control of a General named Idi Amin Dada. What is he like?' Porter said 'General Amin's gone on record as saying he loves Canada and the Commonwealth. He also vowed that his country of Uganda would have democratic elections soon. The British and Americans have recognized him as the Ugandan government and so do we.'"[10]

The nationalizations during Obote's first turn at governance were perceived as a threat to Western corporate interests that were established in Uganda during British rule. Additionally, Obote carried the pan-Africanist torch at a time of Western, including Canadian, support for the apartheid regimes in Southern Africa. As a result, Ottawa heaved a sigh of relief at Obote's demise. The immediate result was Idi Amin's violent and maniacal regime.

CHILE, 1973

On September 11, 1973, the democratically elected president of Chile, Salvador Allende, was overthrown by General Augusto Pinochet. In the aftermath, 3,000 leftists were murdered, tens of thousands tortured and hundreds of thousands driven from the country. Allende's Marxist policies, including the nationalization of some mining operations in Chile, were nullified as Pinochet laid the ground for the first "neoliberal" economy in the Western Hemisphere.

Allende gave the lie to Western propaganda that Marxist governments were inherently violent, undemocratic, and authoritarian. His Popular Unity party did not achieve power through armed revolution, but at the ballot box. This worried the US and its allies immensely. "In world opinion," Chilean documentarian Patricio Guzmán stated, "Allende represented a new and different political way" that threated transnational capital.[1]

In 1972, Allende spoke at the United Nations to denounce the growing unaccountability of Western multinationals around the globe. Allende told the UN:

> We are faced by a direct confrontation between the large transnational corporations and the states. The corporations are interfering in the fundamental political, economic and military decisions of the states. The

corporations are global organizations that do not depend on any state and whose activities are not controlled by, nor are they accountable to any parliament or any other institution representative of the collective interest. ... The large transnational firms are prejudicial to the genuine interests of the developing countries and their dominating and uncontrolled action is also carried out in the industrialized countries, where they are based.[2]

A year later the Pierre Trudeau government welcomed Allende's violent death in a military coup that brought seventeen years of brutal military dictatorship to Chile.

From diplomatic isolation to economic asphyxiation, Ottawa's policy towards Allende's Chile was clear. Ottawa was hostile to Allende's program from the start. In 1964, Eduardo Frei defeated Allende in presidential elections. Worried about growing support for socialism, Ottawa gave $8.6 million to Frei's Chile, its first aid to a South American country.[3] When Allende won the next election, Trudeau refused to travel to Chile to meet Allende. After his victory, Allende invited Trudeau to visit Santiago, but Ottawa refused "for fear of alienating rightist elements in Chile and elsewhere."[4] Additionally, Canadian assistance disappeared. Export Development Canada (EDC) also refused to finance Canadian exports to Chile, which contributed to a reduction in trade between the two countries. The suspension of EDC credits led Chile's minister of finance to criticize Canada's "banker's attitude."[5] But suspending bilateral assistance and export insurance was not enough. In 1972, Ottawa joined Washington in voting to cut off all money from the International Monetary Fund (IMF) to the Chilean government (when Allende was first elected, Western banks, including Canada's, withdrew from Chile).

While Trudeau collaborated with the US in its attacks on the Chilean economy, he maintained ties with the white supremacist regimes in Southern Africa. Tyler Shipley explains: "In 1971, while Canada was turning off the faucet for Chile, Trudeau's external affairs minister insisted that Canada's 'capacity to influence' the white minorities in Southern Africa was limited and that more economic connection—not less—was the best way to exert pressure for change."[6] In short, Trudeau dismissed aid boycotts against white supremacist regimes in Southern Africa as ineffective while imposing a similar strategy on an elected socialist government in Latin America.

When the coup against Allende finally occurred on September 11, 1973, the repression was immediate. The National Stadium in Santiago was converted into an open-air prison where those suspected of leftist sympathies were tortured and killed in front of their fellow prisoners. Tens of thousands of Allende supporters were terrorized or murdered.

Days after Pinochet ousted Allende, Andrew Ross, Canada's ambassador to Chile cabled External Affairs: "Reprisals and searches have created panic atmosphere affecting particularly expatriates including the *riffraff of the Latin American Left* to whom Allende gave asylum … the country has been on a prolonged political binge under the elected Allende government and the junta has assumed the probably thankless task of *sobering Chile up.*" Thousands were incarcerated, tortured, and killed in "sobering Chile up."

Within three weeks of the coup, Canada recognized Pinochet's military junta. Ross stated· "I can see no useful purpose to withholding recognition unduly. Indeed, such action might even tend to delay Chile's eventual return to the democratic process." Pinochet would not step down for seventeen years.

Diplomatic support for Pinochet led to economic assistance. Just after the coup, Canada voted for a $22 million ($100 million in today's money) Inter-American Development Bank loan "rushed through the bank with embarrassing haste." Ottawa immediately endorsed sending $95 million from the IMF to Chile and supported renegotiating the country's debt held by the Paris Club. After refusing to provide credits to the elected government, on October 2, 1973, EDC announced it was granting $5 million in credit to Chile's central bank to purchase six Twin Otter aircraft from De Havilland, which could carry troops to and from short makeshift strips.

Right after the coup the World Bank chose Noranda Inc. to assess Chile's mining laws. Noranda was chosen because it was a Canadian rather than US corporation. Noranda was also the first foreign company to announce plans to invest in Pinochet's Chile. *El Mercurio* newspaper noted, "the agreement reached with Noranda mines, in the present national and international conjunction, reiterates the confidence that foreign investors are demonstrating towards our country."

Timothy David Clark describes mining as "the motor of [Chile's] development and party to its plunder."[7] Pinochet gave massive concessions to transnational mining companies, including those based in Canada.

By 1978, Canadian support for the coup d'état was significant. It included:

- Support for $810 million in multilateral loans with Canada's share amounting to about $40 million.
- Five EDC facilities worth between $15 and $30 million.
- Two Canadian debt re-scheduling for Chile, equivalent to additional loans of approximately $5 million.
- Twenty loans by Canadian chartered banks worth more than $100 million, including a 1977 loan by Toronto Dominion to DINA (Pinochet's secret police) to purchase equipment.
- Direct investments by Canadian companies valued at nearly $1 billion.

A 1976 Latin America Working Group Letter noted, "Canadian economic relations, in the form of bank loans, investments and government supported financial assistance have helped consolidate the Chilean dictatorship and, by granting it a mantle of respectability and financial endorsation [sic], have encouraged its continued violation of human rights."[8]

Canadian leftists were outraged at Ottawa's support for the coup and its unwillingness to accept refugees hunted by the military regime. Many denounced the federal government's policy and some occupied various Chilean and Canadian government offices in protest. The federal government was surprised at the scope of the opposition, which curtailed some support for the junta. A 1974 cabinet document lamented that "the attention... focused on the Chilean Government's use of repression against its opponents has led to an unfavourable reaction among the Canadian public—a reaction which will not permit any significant increase in Canadian aid to this country."[9]

Jan Raska writes: "Aware of American support for the new Pinochet government and uncertain about the political affiliation of the aforementioned refugees the Canadian government acted slowly for nearly a year before implementing rigid security screening to prevent communist sympathizers from entering Canada."[10] It was only after years of lobbying from the United Nations High Commissioner for Refugees, Amnesty International, Canadian churches, and activist organisations that the Trudeau government sought to placate protesters by granting 7,000 refugees from Pinochet's regime asylum in Canada.[11] But they continued to support the dictatorship directly responsible for the refugee problem.

PERU, 1992

In April 1992, Canada refused to condemn Peruvian president Alberto Fujimori's coup against Peru's elected congress, sometimes dubbed the "autogolpe" or "self-coup." The coup was a way for Fujimori to push through neoliberal economic reforms and empower the military, police, and National Intelligence Service (SIN).

On April 5, the Peruvian military took control of "Lima's streets, the Congress, and the Palace of Justice, television and radio stations, newspaper and magazine offices, and some party and union headquarters." Fujimori then broadcast to the nation that the military coup was required to replace the "chaos and corruption" and the "existing institutional order," which had been rendered dysfunctional by "party elites."[1]

Fujimori organized the coup with Vladimiro Montesinos, his SIN chief and a long-time CIA contact, and elements within the military that supported a Pinochet-style regime. After the coup, Fujimori granted greater impunity to Peruvian soldiers combatting rural guerrillas, which led to a huge increase in sexual violence by state forces.[2]

Fujimori had tacit or overt support from much of the military and business sectors and from Washington. Overall, economic elites in Peru "expressed overwhelming support for Fujimori's actions after the coup," and "[s]everal business association leaders attended the swearing-in ceremony for the new cabinet" the day after the coup.[3][4] Following a coup that granted Fujimori "complete dictatorial powers," Washington and the OAS publicly urged the president to restore representative democracy. But this was a formality since they took no other action.

Canada, meanwhile, did not issue a clear-cut statement of condemnation. On April 6, Bill Fairbairn of the Inter-Church Committee on Human Rights in Latin America sent a letter to external affairs secretary Barbara McDougall calling on Ottawa to condemn Fujimori's actions. On April 7, McDougall released a statement noting "concern" about the events in Peru.

That concern dissipated as Peru became one of Canada's closest business partners on the continent. In collaboration with the World Bank, Fujimori instituted a structural reform program that opened huge areas of Peruvian natural resources to foreign companies. "In 1991," writes José De Echave, "registered mining rights covered 2,258,000 hectares; in 1997—a peak year—they reached 15,597,000 hectares."[5] During the early 1990s Canadian mining holdings in Peru grew from three to 98 properties.[6]

When the leftist Túpac Amaru guerrilla group took dozens of foreign diplomats hostage at the Japanese Embassy in Lima in 1996, Canadian JTF2 special forces reportedly participated in the US-led rescue effort. It left all fourteen guerrillas dead, including many of them reportedly executed.

In 1998, Fujimori came to Canada on a four-day state visit "aimed at boosting trade relations between Canada and Peru." Activists and human rights groups urged prime minister Jean Chrétien to speak out about Fujimori's abuses, but Chrétien refused to do so. Instead, he stood next to Fujimori at a joint press conference, assured the press they had "already discussed the issue," and allowed Fujimori to make the outlandish claim that "fortunately we have arrived to the point (in Peru) where human rights are respected."[7]

After ten years Fujimori stepped down in 2000 following an election that was so blatantly rigged that he lost US and OAS support. When US and Canadian officials shunned Fujimori's third inauguration ceremony, his days were numbered and months later he agreed to a transition of power.

Much of the economic foundations of Canada's modern investments in Peru were laid in the aftermath of Fujimori's April 1992 coup d'état.

RUSSIA, 1993

On October 4, 1993, Russian president Boris Yeltsin bombed his own country's parliament building, the White House. The aim was to end an elected, constitutional force's opposition to his unilateral reforms. Ottawa effectively backed an anti-parliamentary coup that left hundreds of anti-Yeltsin protestors dead.[1]

The conflict between the executive branch and parliament (Supreme Soviet) began as a result of the destruction wrought by Yeltsin's Western-backed "shock therapy." The neoliberal economic reforms laid waste to Russian society, impoverishing the vast majority while enriching a handful of well-connected insiders.[2] The pain of shock therapy spurred opposition to Yeltsin.

At the start of 1993 parliamentary resistance to Yeltsin radicalized and by October, Russia was embroiled in what Boris Kagarlitsky called "a minor civil war."[3] In that war, Canada sided with Yeltsin who consolidated power in the presidency.

In September 1993 the clash between Yeltsin and Parliament intensified when he dissolved Parliament, suspended numerous articles of the constitution, and inaugurated presidential rule. The Constitutional Court and legislature accused Yeltsin of a coup, removed him from the presidency, and named vice president Aleksandr Rutskoi acting president.

In early October 1993, supporters of the Parliament occupied government buildings, including the mayor's office and the Ostankino TV station. In response, Yeltsin cut off power, water, and electricity to the Parliament building. He ordered the military to attack pro-democracy protestors, bomb the White House with heavy artillery, and storm the battered building. Fifteen hundred people were killed in the fighting according to the defenders of the parliament (140 according to the government).[4]

After rolling over the elected parliament, Yeltsin restricted the opposition press and banned numerous political parties and organizations. After polls suggested the Communist Party would win, he also invited the US to rig the 1996 presidential elections.

Ottawa offered no condemnation of the deadly coup. Instead, it increased its collaboration with the Yeltsin regime.

From the beginning, Ottawa backed Yeltsin with advisers and hundreds of millions of dollars in assistance. In his memoirs, former prime minister Brian Mulroney boasted that "on a percentage basis" only Germany had provided more aid to Yeltsin's Russia than Canada.[5] As Mulroney's ambassador to Russia, Jeremy Kinsman, wrote, "We Canadians gave whole-hearted support to Russian reformers. We flew in our expensive bankers, legal experts, parliamentarians and top bureaucrats to teach them how we do things." Canada's "whole-hearted support" included "hugely ambitious aid projects to privatize collective farms, teach fledgling provincial parliamentarians about fiscal federalism and write laws on copyright." Lavishing praise on Yeltsin, Kinsman added that he "gave paramount importance to simple, basic new rights—real votes, home ownership, free speech."[6]

In April 1993, prime minister Brian Mulroney and US president Bill Clinton met Yeltsin and voiced support for his reforms. At the meeting, Mulroney committed another $200 million in "economic and technical aid" to Russia.[7]

Later in 1993, new Canadian prime minister Kim Campbell met Yeltsin and praised his actions. In her memoirs, Campbell described him as "a giant" who was "trying to create democracy and a modern economy in Russia."[8]

Canada played a significant role in promoting the post-Soviet neoliberal economy. To spur economic liberalization, Ottawa granted subsidies to Canadian companies investing in Russia.[9] Canadian firms became major players in the oil sector.

They feared the Russian parliament's ambivalence towards shock therapy.[10] Carl H. McMillan explains, "the former Russian parliament gave consideration to amending the law on foreign investment to place conditions on concession contracts to foreign companies in the oil and other extractive industries," which prompted Canadian oil firms to consider "retrenching or withdrawing."[11]

After he bombed his parliament and assumed greater presidential powers, Western aid and investment grew and Yeltsin continued to be a guest of honour at G7 meetings. In 1995, prime minister Jean Chrétien invited Yeltsin to participate in the G7 in Halifax, Nova Scotia.[12] His supposed reputation as a democrat and modernizer were constantly reinforced in Western press coverage. In Kagarlitsky's words, Yeltsin "got away with everything—the destruction of the Soviet Union, the collapse of industry, a drastic fall in living standards, the lost war in Chechnya, and corruption scandals in his own family."[13]

In the apparent name of democracy, Ottawa supported a presidential coup and bombing of an elected parliament.

HAITI, 2004

On February 29, 2004, Canadian special forces "secured" the airport from which Haiti's elected president Jean-Bertrand Aristide was bundled ("kidnapped" in his words) onto a plane by US Marines. He was deposited against his will in the Central African Republic. Almost immediately after Aristide was removed, 500 Canadian troops were dispatched to patrol the streets of Port-Au-Prince.

Aristide's overthrow was the culmination of a US-led and Canadian-supported destabilization campaign that included "civil society building," military and paramilitary interventions, an aid embargo that would cripple the country's economy, a full-scale disinformation campaign waged by Haitian elite-owned and international corporate media, and concerted diplomatic efforts directed at guaranteeing regime change would be both acceptable to the international community and believable to a confused public.

Aristide, who had lived and studied in Montréal for three years, rose to prominence as a leader in the movement that toppled the thirty-year reign of "Papa Doc" and "Baby Doc" Duvalier. The slightly built former priest's political philosophy was rooted in liberation theology. During his first term in office, he raised the minimum wage, invested in education, and elevated the Creole language from its underclass status. Aristide promoted a modest program of favouring the impoverished majority in his second term. His redistributionist policies angered the small number of families who run the economy and his call for France to repay its $21 billion ransom/debt of independence angered Paris and others.

Incredibly, the 2004 coup against Aristide began with an effort to discredit elections he neither participated in nor oversaw. In the May 2000 legislative and municipal elections, Aristide's Fanmi Lavalas won more than 70% of the vote. They took an unprecedented 89 of 115 mayoral positions, 72 of 83 seats in the Chamber of Deputies and 18 of 19 Senate seats. Immediately afterwards, OAS observers called the elections "a great success for the Haitian population, which turned out in large and orderly numbers to choose both their local and national governments."[1] According to the OAS, 60% of registered voters went to the polls and there were "very few"[2] incidents of either fraud or violence.

In response to its crushing defeat, the opposition accused the electoral commission of organizing a "massive fraud." Realizing there was little chance Fanmi Lavalas would be defeated at the ballot box in the foreseeable future, the US and Canadian-dominated OAS Observation Mission legitimated the opposition's protests. The OAS challenged the calculation of majorities in some Senate seats, claiming Lavalas should have only won seven senate seats in the first round, not the sixteen announced by the electoral council.

The electoral council determined the 50% plus one vote required for a first-round victory by calculating the percentages of the top four candidates. The OAS contended that the count should include all candidates. However, OAS concerns were disingenuous since they worked with the electoral council to prepare the elections and were aware of the counting method beforehand. The same procedure was used in prior elections, but they failed to voice any concerns until Lavalas' landslide victory. Finally, the tabulation method proposed by the OAS would probably not have altered the outcome of the senate seats.

In effect, the OAS jumped on a technicality in the counting of some Senate seats to subsequently characterize an election for 7000 positions "deeply flawed."

The Canadian government played an important role in the OAS electoral mission. Ottawa put up more than $300,000 for the OAS Observation Mission and many Canadians were part of it.[2] [3] [4]

Canada worked to discredit the May 2000 election outside of the OAS structure as well. Ottawa supported some in the opposition's demand for a "revision" of the elections.[5] A week after the election, Foreign Affairs dispatched its top diplomat on Haiti, David Lee, alongside US counterpart, Donald Steinberg, to meet Haiti's electoral council to review the partial results. In response, the Rally of Organizations for Change accused Canadian officials of "interference in Haitian elections."[6]

A participant in the electoral observation mission, the president of Québec's National Assembly,

Jean-Pierre Charbonneau, told *La Presse*, "the Haitian authorities must make the required corrections and if the PFL [Fanmi Lavalas] is really as strong as it says it is, it should not fear a transparent and legitimate process."

Canada and the US threatened to cut off assistance to the country to protest the formula used to determine the winners of the senate seats.[7] In September 2000, foreign affairs minister Lloyd Axworthy and US secretary of state Madeleine Albright convened a meeting of "the friends of Haiti." The meeting resulted in a US declaration that they would withdraw assistance for Haiti's November presidential election. Ottawa also decided not to finance or participate in the observer mission to the presidential election.[8]

Polls predicted a landslide victory for Aristide. A USAID poll of 1002 Haitians conducted nationwide by CID-Gallup in October 2000 showed 92.8% of those surveyed knew about the upcoming presidential election and the vast majority said they were very likely (55.9%) or somewhat likely (22.7%) to vote. Over 50% chose Aristide as the most trusted leader and no member of the opposition came anywhere near that figure. Lavalas was the preferred party by an incredible thirteen to one.

Unsurprisingly, Aristide won the subsequent poll with 92% of the vote. Though most of the opposition parties boycotted the presidential poll, no analyst seriously doubted Aristide's overwhelming popularity. Haitian officials and some 3000 independent observers reported that over four million voters (more than half the population) registered, 60% of whom voted. These figures were better than the 2000 US election and Aristide's 92% of the vote was proportionally almost double what George W. Bush received that same month.

The Republican takeover of the presidency hardened US policy towards Haiti's impoverished majority. Bush appointed a coterie of anti-Aristide extremists, including neoconservative Roger Noriega, who was named US ambassador to the OAS. From that position, Noriega worked closely on Haiti with Canadian OAS ambassador David Lee. As Carlo Dade of the Canadian Foundation for the Americas explained after the 2004 coup, "the Aristide regime was doomed with the 2000 elections in the United States. The United States government had an active policy of supporting the opposition in undermining Aristide."[9]

Given Aristide's electoral victory, the "international community" had little choice but to recognize him as legitimately elected. But at Aristide's first international event, prime minister Jean Chrétien reportedly "lectured" him on the "shortcomings" of the May elections. At the April 2001 Summit of the Americas in Québec City, Lavalas was blamed for failing "to end the deadlock in negotiations with opposition parties that followed last year's elections, which were widely condemned as flawed."[10] Chrétien said the heads of state would pay special attention to Haiti and called for greater intervention by the US and Canadian-dominated OAS. Canada's prime minister asked the secretary general of the OAS, César Gaviria, to visit Port-au-Prince and to work with CARICOM to deal with the Haitian "crisis." In response to Chrétien's request, the prime minister of Barbados, Owen Arthur, visited Port-au-Prince and subsequently the OAS appointed a special representative for the reinforcement of democracy in Haiti, Canadian diplomat David Lee.[11] The US largely funded Lee's mission in Haiti.[12]

Chrétien pressured Aristide to negotiate with the opposition, putting the onus on him to resolve the dispute over the May 2000 elections. But, even after Aristide caved to pressure and convinced multiple Fanmi Lavalas senators to resign, the destabilization campaign continued. As part of the destabilization campaign against Aristide's government, the donors sought to strangle the country economically. At the behest of the US and Canada, the World Bank and Inter-American Development Bank blocked $500 million in already approved loans.[13] These loans were equivalent to over half the Haitian government's annual budget. According to economist Jeffrey Sachs, the loan and aid cut-off had the effect of "squeezing Haiti's economy dry and causing untold suffering for its citizens." Once Aristide took office, Canadian aid to the country dropped by more than half and the funds going to the government all but dried up.

Concurrently, the US and Canada united the political opposition. The dilemma for the North American "democracy promoters," according to a US official interviewed by journalist Anthony Fenton, was "a very weak opposition, a very fragmented opposition with no platform, unwilling to come together and form some sort of coalition by ideology or program or anything … Aristide really had 70% of the popular support and then the 120 other parties had the 30% split in one hundred and twenty different ways, which is basically impossible to compete [with]."[14]

Under the guidance of the International Republican Institute, a US government agency affiliated with the Republican Party, an eclectic mix of social democratic, neo-Duvalierist, right-wing fundamentalist Christian, and business-linked parties merged to create the Convergence Démocratique (CD). The CD demanded that the May 2000 elections be annulled, that Aristide resign and that the military be revived. Washington and Ottawa insisted the elected government reach a settlement with CD over the "disputed" May elections before they would restore aid. Privately, however, they instructed CD leaders to maintain their intransigent attitude.

Due to the unpopularity of the defeated political opposition, the US, Canada, and the EU also funded a parallel "independent" civic opposition movement. They funnelled money to "human rights, democracy, and good governance" projects that fueled vociferous NGO criticism of alleged human rights abuses by the Lavalas government. Groups were funded to produce radio shows claiming the elections had been "fraudu-lent," unite opponents of the "dictatorship," and organize anti-government demonstrations. Between 2000-2002, according to a Canadian International Development Agency (CIDA) report, its spending "was characterized by a shift in support to civil society." CIDA spent $67.3 million in Haiti, which was largely channeled to NGOs. Though this funding was ostensibly "apolitical," virtually without exception Haitian organizations receiving CIDA funding—either directly or indirectly via Canadian NGOs—opposed Aristide.

In a December 2004 assessment of Canada's "difficult partnership" with Haiti, CIDA remarked that by "engaging a coalition of key players" and "providing sufficient resources," Canada's support for "civil society initiatives and Canadian NGO partners produced relatively good qualitative results." The shift to civil society "contributed to building the capacity of non-governmental actors to generate grassroots demand for reform."[15]

As one example, CIDA-funded Development & Peace assisted its Haitian NGO partners "to become players to be reckoned with and to help put an end to the political chaos caused by the current regime." Through its Haitian partners, Development & Peace spent $1.4 million in Haiti from 2000-2003 working with over 70 local organizations "to improve the ... external circulation of information" and "to develop action and training plans, and to mobilize." Development & Peace also organized a national symposium on strategies for fighting the "dictatorship" that was attended by representatives of forty Haitian groups. The symposium led to the creation of several regional networks of groups opposed to the government, which "started coordinating their activities closely to develop synergy in action."

USAID also channeled tens of millions of dollars into unifying and galvanizing "civil society" opposition to Aristide's government. Students, women, and union organizers in Jacmel told a US human rights delegation that USAID "trained us and taught us how to organize, and we organized the groups you see here to demand the corrupt government of Aristide be brought down."

In December 2002, the crown jewel of the "civic" wing of the opposition was unveiled. The Group of 184 presented itself as a broad-based citizens movement encompassing 184 organizations representing human rights groups, women, peasants, labour, intellectuals, students, and more. Claims of pluralism notwithstanding, the Group of 184 was dominated by a small segment of Haitian society. The Group of 184 grew out of the Initiative de la Société Civile, "a collection of business and religious elite organisations" funded by USAID and CIDA which, according to the UK-based Haiti Support Group, was "wholly unrepresentative of the Haitian majority." Light-skinned sweatshop industrialists who opposed raising the minimum wage, Andy Apaid Jr. and Charles Henri Baker, dominated the Group of 184's leadership.

Lawyer and human rights researcher Thomas Griffin described how the Group of 184 grew out of USAID-funded groups like the International Foundation for Electoral Systems (IFES), which invested millions in building up the "civic opposition." A University of Miami Human Rights Investigation explained that IFES:

> [F]ormulated groups that never existed, united pre-existing groups, gave them sensitization seminars, paid for people to attend, paid for entertainment and catering, and basically built group after group. ... They reached out to student groups, business ... [and] human rights groups—which they actually paid off to report human rights atrocities to make Aristide look bad. ... They bought journalists, and the IFES associations grew into the Group of 184 that became a solidified opposition against Aristide.

Ottawa supported the Group of 184 and its member organizations. CIDA spent $13 million on "civil society, democracy and human rights" themed projects implemented by NGOs affiliated with the Group of 184 and Canadian aid money helped pay to elaborate the Group of 184's "social contract."

The Group of 184 and CD staged numerous demonstrations denouncing the government and calling for Aristide to resign. Students at the State University (where many foreign funded NGO leaders worked as professors) turned against the government. Clashes between pro- and anti-government demonstrators became increasingly frequent, as pro-Lavalas popular organizations mobilized to counter (typically much less numerous) Group of 184 demonstrators. Violent confrontations escalated from stone throwing to attacks with weapons, and on rare occasions firearms. Tensions led to isolated cases of political killings, such as the murder of journalist Brignol Lindor by members of a pro-Lavalas group, in response to the killing of one of their members by opposition supporters in Petit Goave. As political scientist Robert Fatton Jr. argued, some pro-Lavalas popular organizations began "threatening the opposition because they believe that it is purposefully exacerbating the crisis to generate a chaos that would nurture the return of the military."

The popular organizations' concerns were not theoretical. In July and December 2001, former soldiers attempted to overthrow Aristide. They conducted a low-level war against the government and its supporters through cross-border raids from the Dominican Republic. The wealthy elite and leading members of the CD secretly bankrolled the "insurgency," which combined former soldiers of the disbanded military and notorious FRAPH leaders such as Louis-Jodel Chamblain.

When pro-Lavalas popular organizations clashed with anti-government protesters, the civic and political opposition accused the government of using gangs to crack down on dissent. The opposition also cited gang violence and drug trafficking as further evidence of the nefarious designs of the Lavalas government and its supporters. These problems, however, afflicted the country—especially Port-au-Prince's fast-growing slums—before and after Aristide's second mandate. Government supporters from the slums were relentlessly demonized as "chimères" (thugs) and "Lavalassian hordes." Some members of the civic and political opposition called Aristide a "fascist" and claimed his government was committing "genocide."

Less partisan observers found that the systematic human rights violations and political repression that characterized the Duvalier dictatorship and military juntas was completely absent. In the context of rising political tensions, cross-border paramilitary attacks and foreign economic strangulation, Amnesty International's reports showed that at most 30 political murders could be attributed to the police or pro-Lavalas groups (only tenuously linked to the government). There was no basis for comparison with previous (or subsequent) governments. According to Peter Hallward, "remember the basic numbers: perhaps 50,000 dead under the Duvaliers (1957-1986), perhaps 700 to 1,000 dead under Namphy/Avril (1986-1990), 4,000 dead under Cedras (1991-1994) and then at least another 3,000 killed under Latortue (2004-2006)." Human rights lawyer Brian Concannon Jr. argued that the opposition's claims of political persecution simply did not align with the reality on the ground:

> The press was so free in [Aristide's second] term that in the lead up to the coup d'état of 2004 you had the press openly calling for the overthrow of the government. In the US, that would not be tolerated. That would be beyond free speech. My expectation is that it would be illegal in Canada as well. There was immense freedom of assembly. There were assemblies that would definitely have been controlled in the U.S. or Canada because they were violent and illegal. But because they were done by the opposition, the Aristide government didn't touch

them. So it's curious that someone like that is called a dictator.

Even with massive funding, the anti-government opposition could not expand its support beyond a small urban, "middle class" base. "Everybody knows that Aristide was bad," explained Paul Farmer. "Everybody, that is, except the Haitian poor—85% of the population." Aristide's popularity remained solid in spite of a deteriorating economic situation and relentless vilification by NGOs and the political opposition. Polls commissioned by USAID from 2002 and 2003 obtained by *New York Times* journalist Tracy Kidder showed consistent popular support for Aristide. Six months after the coup, a poll "showed that Aristide was still the only figure in Haiti with a favourability rating above 50%," admitted US ambassador James Foley in a confidential cable.[16]

Group of 184 demonstrations were regularly dwarfed by pro-Lavalas counter-rallies. By the end of 2003, the artificially inflated opposition movement had managed to turn only a small segment of the population against the government. "To the distress of the Group of Friends [Canada, US and France]," observed David Malone of Foreign Affairs Canada, "Aristide remains the most potent political force in Haiti." The NGOs, Group of 184, and CD could not mount a serious political challenge to the government. They required direct intervention from the imperial triumvirate and their Canadian NGO partners legitimated the US, French, and Canadian invasion.

A couple of days before Aristide took office in 2001, the federal government's arm's-length human rights organization Rights & Democracy noted, "Aristide's election came amidst widespread doubts about his own and the Préval government's commitment to democracy." A year later, Rights & Democracy claimed, "the elected officials of the Lavalas Family and representatives of 'popular organizations' close to that party are often implicated in the most flagrant violation of Haitian laws." Five months before the coup, Rights & Democracy released a report that described Haiti's pro-coup Group of 184 as "grassroots" and a "promising civil society movement."

Many Canadian NGOs called for Aristide's overthrow. On December 15, 2003, Québec's NGO umbrella group, Association québécoise des organismes de coopération internationale (AQOCI), called for the Canadian government to "publicly denounce" Aristide and his "regime," which was "rife with human rights abuses." Development & Peace went even further in a December 16, 2003 letter to prime minister Paul Martin, calling on Canada to demand that Aristide resign and to help put in place an international force to disarm Aristide's supporters.

Two months later the Concertation Pour Haiti (CPH), an informal group of half a dozen NGOs including Development and Peace, AQOCI, and Entraide Missionaire, branded Aristide a "tyrant," his government a "dictatorship" and "regime of terror," and called for Aristide's removal.

The NGOs were pushing on an open door. On January 31 and February 1, 2003, Ottawa played an important role in consolidating the international forces that would carry out the coup. Jean Chrétien's government organized the "Ottawa Initiative on Haiti" to discuss that country's future. No Haitian officials were invited to this assembly where high-level US, Canadian and French officials decided the elected president "must go," the army be recreated and the country put under a Kosovo-like UN trusteeship.

Present at the Ottawa Initiative discussion were Canadian health (and later foreign) minister Pierre Pettigrew, US assistant secretary of state for the Western Hemisphere, Otto Reich, another state department official, Mary Ellen Gilroy, assistant secretary general of the Organization of American States, Luigi Einaudi, El Salvador's foreign minister Maria de Avila, and France's minister of security and conflict prevention Pierre-André Wiltzer. They were all invited to the government's Meech Lake Conference Centre in Gatineau, Québec by secretary of state for Latin America and minister for La Francophonie Denis Paradis.

The late prominent journalist Michel Vastel brought the gathering to public attention in the March 15, 2003, issue of *L'actualité*, Québec's equivalent to *Maclean's*. In an article titled "Haiti put under U.N. Tutelage?" Vastel wrote that the possibility of Aristide's departure, a potential trusteeship and the return of Haiti's military were discussed.[17] After the coup, Vastel said his source on this private conference was his friend Denis Paradis and information on the meeting was corroborated by French officials. For his part, Paradis would deny Vastel's account of the "Ottawa Initiative on Haiti," but the story was never retracted by Vastel or *L'actualité*. In several post-coup interviews, Vastel stood behind his original article and asserted that several follow-up meetings took place involving the same participants, as well as US secretary of state Colin Powell.

While claiming he was misinterpreted by Vastel, Paradis made it clear that a foreign intervention into Haiti was discussed at the "Ottawa Initiative on Haiti." In a September 2004 interview with researcher Anthony Fenton, Paradis explained, "there was one thematic that went under the whole meeting … the responsibility to protect." A showpiece of the Liberals' foreign policy, the responsibility to protect doctrine asserts that where gross human rights abuses are occurring, it is the duty of the international community to intervene, over and above considerations of state sovereignty. In a highly censored February 11, 2004 cable from the Canadian Embassy in Port-au-Prince to Foreign Affairs, ambassador Kenneth Cook explained, "President Aristide is clearly a serious aggravating factor in the current crisis" and there is a need to "consider the options including whether a case can be made for the duty [responsibility] to protect." According to an Access to Information request, Foreign Affairs monitored public reaction to Vastel's story. In an e-mail exchange with Foreign Affairs, Canada's ambassador to Haiti, Kenneth Cook, pointed out that of the seventy letters received by *L'actualité* on the topic of regime change, "most were positive." As such, one suspects that Paradis' leak to Vastel was a trial balloon designed to gauge the response of the opposition parties, Haitian community, and other social organizations.

For obvious reasons, the Haitian government wasn't too pleased with the meeting. Days after it came to public attention, Haiti's foreign minister demanded a meeting with Canada's ambassador, while Haiti's Radio Metropole reported that Paradis sent a letter to Haiti's foreign minister telling him the Ottawa meeting posed no threat to his government.

Alongside international diplomatic efforts and civil society opposition, a low-intensity war was waged against the government. Dozens of Lavalas members and supporters were killed in Belladere and other towns on the border with the Dominican Republic between 2001 and 2003.[18] On July 28, 2001, several police stations were attacked. In a more serious coup attempt, more than three dozen gunmen stormed the national palace on December 17, 2001. With a helicopter and 50-mm-caliber machine gun, they killed four and briefly occupied the building. Five attackers were killed by police. The attackers announced via radio that Aristide was no longer president and that Guy Philippe now commanded the police.[19] The attack was reportedly prepared in Santo Domingo by former police chiefs Philippe and Jean-Jacques Nau.

Philippe and four others, including Paul Arcelin, were later arrested by Dominican authorities. A

Dominican military official told the Associated Press, "these people are being investigated because of allegations that they are trying to reach Haiti with the aim of conspiring" against the elected government. Arcelin's relationship with Philippe revealed the connection between the paramilitaries and the Convergence Démocratique. Arcelin was the CD representative in the Dominican Republic.

Arcelin appears to have been working with the International Republican Institute (IRI). In a July 2004 *Salon* article, Max Blumenthal wrote:

> Others describe more formal ties between IRI and the insurgents. Jean Michel Caroit, chief correspondent in the Dominican Republic for the French daily *Le Monde*, says he saw Philippe's political advisor, Paul Arcelin, at an IRI meeting at Hotel Santo Domingo in December 2003. Caroit, who was having drinks in the lobby with several attendees, said the meeting was convened 'quite discreetly.' His account dovetailed with that of a Haitian journalist who told *Salon* on condition of anonymity that Arcelin often attended IRI meetings in Santo Domingo as Convergence's representative to the Dominican Republic.

A former professor at the Université du Québec à Montréal, Arcelin later proclaimed himself "intellectual author" and "political leader" of the military uprising that ousted Aristide. Just after the coup, the *Montréal Gazette* reported, "Arcelin, a rebel and self-proclaimed architect of the 2004 coup d'état, does not hesitate to express his role in Aristide's overthrow, describing phone calls made from Canada to rebel leader Guy Philippe in Haiti in order to discuss coup strategy."[20]

Arcelin told the *Gazette*, "two years ago, I met Guy Philippe in Santo Domingo and we spent 10 to 15 hours a day together, plotting against Aristide." He added, "from time to time we'd [Arcelin and Philippe] cross the border clandestinely through the woods to conspire against Aristide, to meet with the opposition."

The *Gazette* also revealed that Arcelin had met Pierre Pettigrew in early February 2004 in Montréal: "He took advantage of the visit and the political clout of his sister-in-law [former Conservative MP Nicole Arcelin-Roy] to meet with Health Minister Pierre Pettigrew. ... 'I explained the reality of Haiti to him,' Arcelin said, pulling Pettigrew's business card out of his wallet. 'He promised to make a report to the Canadian government about what I had said.'"

At the end of 2003, Philippe and the former soldiers intensified their cross-border attacks against government targets. They were subsequently joined by a coalition of gangs in Gonaïves led by a former death squad leader. On February 5, 2004, the insurgents seized Gonaïves, the country's fourth largest city. The heavily armed force rampaged across Haiti, killing police, emptying jails, and burning public buildings.

Initially foreign affairs minister Bill Graham denounced the rebellion, saying Canada supported the elected government. "Aristide has been elected and he must complete his term," explained Graham in a mid-January 2004 *La Presse* article titled "Caricom

tells Paul Martin about Aristide's popularity in Haiti."
"If new elections were held today, he would probably
be re-elected."[21]

The Bush Administration publicly responded to
the rebellion in a similar way. In what was probably a
bid to claim deniability and a way to hedge based on
developments, US secretary of state Colin Powell told
a Senate foreign relations committee on February 12,
"the policy of the administration is not regime change.
President Aristide is the elected president of Haiti."
Powell reaffirmed that position five days later: "We
cannot buy into a proposition that says the elected
president must be forced out of office by thugs and
those who do not respect law and are bringing terrible
violence to the Haitian people."

At the same time that they criticized the rebels, US
and Canadian officials strengthened their hand. They
demanded Aristide negotiate with an intransigent political opposition working in parallel with the rebels. In
mid-February 2004, Ottawa sent a delegation to Port-
au-Prince to deliver a "firm message to Mr. Aristide,
that he must respect his obligations," explained
Canada's foreign minister. Graham claimed the mission's objective was "to create a situation where the
opposition can enter into discussions," but the actual
aim was to further weaken the elected government.[22]

On February 22, the insurgents took Cap Haïtien,
the country's second largest city. Scores of police officers were killed and many more simply abandoned
their posts to the better-armed rebels. As the insurgents

made their way to Port-au-Prince, the international community ignored the elected government's requests for "a few dozen" peacekeepers to restore order in a country without an army. On February 26, three days before Aristide's removal, the OAS permanent council called on the UN Security Council to "take all the necessary and appropriate urgent measures to address the deteriorating situation in Haiti." CARICOM called on the UN Security Council to deploy an emergency military task force to assist Aristide's government. This appeal for assistance was flatly rejected by the world's most powerful nations.

By the end of the month, gunmen had overrun all major cities except Port-au-Prince and rebels set up on the outskirts. Supporters of the president built barricades across the capital. They blocked the main arteries of the city of two million and prepared to fight. Even with most of the country in rebel hands, the government's prospects began to improve as pro-government police recaptured several cities. A shipment of guns, bulletproof vests, and ammunition was in Kingston, Jamaica, on route from South Africa at the request of CARICOM. Rumors were swirling that Venezuela had agreed to send soldiers to protect the constitutional government. Most important, Port-au-Prince's size made it difficult to capture for a few hundred men.

But the battle for Port-au-Prince never took place. In the early hours of February 29, 2004, US soldiers, with Canadian forces "securing" the airport, escorted Haiti's elected president and his security staff onto a jet and out of the country. US officials insisted the president had resigned to avoid a bloodbath. This version of events was accepted by most of the world's media despite Aristide's contradictory account.

Prominent professor Jeffrey Sachs recounts the events of February 29:

> According to Mr. Aristide, U.S. officials in Port-au-Prince told him that rebels were on the way to the presidential residence and that he and his family were unlikely to survive unless they immediately boarded a U.S.-chartered plane standing by to take them to exile. The U.S. made it clear, he said, that it would provide no protection for him at the official residence, despite the ease with which this could have been arranged. Indeed, says Aristide's lawyer, the U.S. blocked reinforcement of Aristide's own security detail and refused him entry to the airplane until he signed a letter of resignation. Then Aristide was denied access to a phone for nearly 24 hours and knew nothing of his destination until he was summarily deposited in the Central African Republic.

Despite ignoring appeals for support from CARICOM and the OAS in the preceding days, soon after US/French/Canadian troops ousted the elected government the UN Security Council passed a motion authorizing an intervention. In a three-minute Sunday night meeting—between 9:52 and 9:55 PM, according to the official UN summary—the Security Council "authorized the immediate deployment of [a] Multinational Interim Force for a period of three months to help to secure and stabilize the capital, Port-au-Prince, and elsewhere in the country."

The resolution repeated coup talking points. It noted, "Haiti's political situation became volatile after flawed elections in May 2000" and claimed the intervention was designed "to further the constitutional political process now under way."[23]

Canada played a role in the kidnapping and coup d'état. JTF2 commandos took control of the airport from which Aristide was bundled onto a plane by US Marines.[24] According to AFP, "about 30 Canadian special forces soldiers secured the airport on Sunday [February 29] and two sharpshooters positioned themselves on the top of the control tower."[25] Members of the elite force had reportedly arrived in Port-au-Prince four or five days earlier, ostensibly to protect Canada's embassy and "secure key locations" in the capital. According to the military's account of Operation PRINCIPAL, "more than 100 CF personnel and four CC-130 Hercules aircraft ... assisted with emergency contingency plans and security measures" during the week before the coup.[26]

Canada, along with France and Chile, provided troops for the subsequent US-led and UN-approved Multinational Interim Force (MIF). As part of the force, 500 Canadian troops patrolled the streets of Port-au-Prince.

An interim government was appointed by a council of "wise people" put together by France, Canada, and the USA. The "illegal" interim government was headed by Gérard Latortue, a man from Florida who had not lived in Haiti for fifteen years.

Latortue set about dismantling the modest social programs established during Aristide's second term and many of the achievements of the 1994–2004 democratic period. Subsidies for impoverished farmers were slashed, an adult literacy program was dismantled, and the minimum wage was reduced. Reversing the limited land reform enacted during Préval's government, thousands of peasants in the Artibonite were evicted from their lands by local landlords and their hired thugs who were sometimes supported by police. The interim regime gave large businesses a three-year tax holiday.

Latortue dismissed the Aristide's government's campaign to force France to repay the independence ransom it extorted from Haiti. The de facto prime minister told Reuters, "this [debt restitution] claim was illegal, ridiculous and was made only for political reasons … This matter is closed. What we need now is increased cooperation with France."[27] However, before he was installed, Latortue told the *Miami Herald* that France repaying the debt was "the moral and politically responsible thing to do."

"A Haitian president demands reparations and ends up in exile," declared the front-page of a May 2022 *New York Times*. Solidifying the historical narrative regarding the coup, then French ambassador Thierry Burkhard admitted that Aristide's call for the restitution of Haiti's $21+ billion debt (ransom) of independence partly explained why he was ousted in 2004. Burkhard told *The New York Times* the elected president's removal was "a coup" that was "probably a bit about" Aristide's campaign for France to repay Haiti.[28]

In *Truth to the Powerless: Canada's Role in Dismantling Democracy in Haiti and the Americas*, then defence minister David Pratt said, "Canada, the US, and France did what was necessary in terms of removing him [Aristide] from power." In the 2022 documentary Pratt claimed Haiti's most popular ever politician was ousted because he'd become a "big man" leader responsible for "abuses of power." But Canada's allies in overthrowing Aristide and thousands of other elected officials were light-skinned oligarchs overseeing profoundly inegalitarian racial capitalism and mercenaries with odious histories. Canada's role in Haiti during this period was to help dismantle the elected forces of social and economic change and reinstitute a repressive right-wing state apparatus violently opposed to the demands of the impoverished majority.

Vaudeville

Haiti

he is at war
his mask
is still intact

for the prime
minister it
is vaudeville

on stage he's
a stand-in
for uncle sam

he swears it's
only a joke
a little prank

he's a master
in the art
of blackface

A Poem by Rob Rolfe

PALESTINE, 2006

In January 2006, Hamas won Canadian-monitored and facilitated legislative elections in Palestine. After Israel, Canada was the first country to cut its assistance to the Palestinian Authority (PA). The aid cut-off, which was designed to sow division within Palestinian society, had devastating social effects. "Open warfare among Gazan families a by-product of aid freeze," explained a *Globe and Mail* headline.

Hamas is an Islamist resistance organization founded in 1987 by Sheikh Ahmed Yassin, a paraplegic who was assassinated (along with nine bystanders) by Hellfire missiles from an Israeli gunship in 2004. The Israeli government initially enabled Hamas as an alternative to the Palestine Liberation Organization (PLO) and leftist resistance organizations. Israeli brigadier general Yitzhak Segev told *The New York Times*, Israel "helped finance the Palestinian Islamist movement as a 'counterweight' to the secularists and leftists of the Palestine Liberation Organization and the Fatah party, led by Yasser Arafat." Once Hamas began to represent an actual threat to Israeli supremacy in occupied Palestine, Israel sought to "bomb, besiege, and blockade it out of existence."[1]

When Hamas won the 2006 legislative elections, that campaign intensified with Canadian support.

Israel instituted an economic blockade of Gaza that severely limited the amount of food, water, and energy available because Palestinians voted for the wrong party in elections internationally recognized as free and fair.

In March 2006, Canada became the first donor to suspend aid to the newly Hamas-led Palestine Authority.[2]

In a bid to lessen division and avoid a full-fledged civil war, political factions representing more than 90% of the Palestinian Legislative Council established a unity government in March 2007. Still, Ottawa shunned the new government. "It's our policy to have no contact with members of the government or deputy ministers," said Daniel Dugas, then foreign affairs minister Peter MacKay's director of communications.[3]

When the Palestinian unity government's information minister travelled to Ottawa on a global peace tour, MacKay refused to meet him. Mustafa Barghouti, who represented a secular party, told *Embassy*: "I think the Canadian government is the only government that is taking such a position, except for Israel. Even the United States has sent its consul general [in Jerusalem, Jacob Walles,] to meet with the Palestinian finance minister [Salam Fayyad]." Barghouti had already met the foreign ministers of Sweden and Norway, the secretary-general of the UN and US secretary of state Condoleezza Rice.

Canada's intransigence was designed to sow division within Palestinian society and destroy the unity government. In fact, Washington and Ottawa actually pushed for war between Hamas and Fatah. A senior figure in the Israeli intelligence establishment explained: "Washington did not want a unity government. It wanted Fatah to wreck it and it sent [US Lieutenant-General Keith] Dayton to create and train a force that could overthrow Hamas. When Hamas pre-empts it, everyone cries foul, claiming it's a military putsch by Hamas—but who did the putsch?"[4]

After Hamas officials were ousted from the PA in June 2007, Ottawa restarted diplomatic relations and financial support. "The Government of Canada welcomes the leadership of President Abbas and Prime Minister [Salam] Fayyad in establishing a government that Canada and the rest of the international community can work with," explained MacKay after the unity government's collapse.[5] With Palestinian society divided and a more compliant authority in control of the West Bank, Canada's foreign aid agency CIDA immediately contributed $8 million "in direct support to the new government." Then in December 2007, the Conservatives announced a five-year $300-million aid program to the Palestinians, which was largely designed to serve Israel's interests.[6]

In the short term, the primary aim of Canadian aid was to create a Palestinian security force "to ensure that the PA maintains control of the West Bank against Hamas," as Canadian ambassador to Israel Jon Allen was quoted as saying by the *Canadian Jewish News*. US General Dayton, in charge of organizing a

10,000-member Palestinian security force, even admitted that he was strengthening Mahmoud Abbas' Fatah against Hamas, telling a US audience in May 2009 his force was "working against illegal Hamas activities." According to *Al Jazeera*, between 2007 and early 2011 PA security forces arrested some 10,000 suspected Hamas supporters.[7]

The broader aim of the US-Canada-UK initiated Palestinian security reform was to build a force to patrol Israel's occupation. Like colonial authorities throughout history, Israel looked to compliant locals to take up the occupation's security burden.

Palestinians have not held elections since 2006. President Mahmoud Abbas' mandate expired in 2009, but the PLO Central Council extended his term indefinitely. Still, when Prime Minister Trudeau met Abbas in June 2021, he reportedly "highlighted Canada's dedication to democratic principles and processes."[8]

HONDURAS, 2009

The Harper government tacitly supported the Honduran military's 2009 removal of elected president Manuel Zelaya. Early on June 28, soldiers entered the presidential palace and took a pyjama-clad Zelaya to Costa Rica. Soon after, demonstrators took to the streets and erected blockades calling for the return of the elected president. In response, the military regime imposed martial law in the capital Tegucigalpa. What followed was a period of instability characterized by widespread state and paramilitary violence against journalists, social movements and the political opposition.

Eight hours after Zelaya's ouster, a Foreign Affairs spokesperson told Mexico's *Notimex* that Canada had "no comment" regarding the coup. It was not until basically every country in the hemisphere denounced the coup that Ottawa finally did so. *Notimex* later reported that Canada was the only country in the hemisphere that did not explicitly call for Zelaya's return to power, and on a number of occasions, minister of state of foreign affairs Peter Kent said it was important to take into account the context in which the military overthrew Zelaya, particularly whether he had violated the constitution. Kent was quoted in *The New York Times* saying, "there is a context in which these events [the coup] happened."

Following the 2009 coup, Honduras had the highest homicide rate in the world and, according to Reporters Without Borders, it became the most dangerous country for journalists in the first quarter of 2010.[1] Scores of activists were murdered in the following years, including Lenca land defender Berta Cáceres, who was one of the highest profile activists in Central America.

In the lead up to Zelaya's ouster, the Harper government displayed a clear ambivalence towards the elected president. With political tensions increasing in Honduras, two days before the coup the Organization of American States (OAS) passed a resolution supporting democracy and the rule of law in that country. Ottawa's representative at the meeting remained silent. Early in June, Kent criticized Zelaya saying, "we have concerns with the government of Honduras."[2] Ottawa opposed Zelaya's plan for a non-binding public poll on whether to hold consultations to reopen the constitution, which was written by a military government. Parroting the baseless accusations of the Honduran oligarchy, Kent said: "There are elections coming up this year and we are watching very carefully the behaviour of the government and what seems to be an attempt to amend the constitution to allow consecutive presidencies."

A businessman and Liberal Party member, Zelaya was not a political outsider or a revolutionary leftist. But, to the chagrin of officials in Washington and Ottawa, he increasingly aligned with the left-wing governments that came to power across Latin America in the early 2000s, particularly Hugo Chávez's Venezuela. He also expressed a willingness to make concessions to Honduras' increasingly organized social movements, which angered the entrenched oligarchy. Zelaya made school more accessible, strengthened environmental protections, and increased the minimum wage substantially. He also announced plans to convene a constituent assembly to rewrite the dictatorship-era constitution.

In addition to these measures, Zelaya implemented a moratorium on new mining concessions. This fact likely perturbed the Canadian government, given that, in the words of one Latin American official, "As far as I can tell, the Canadian ambassador here is a representative for Canadian mining companies," which dominated the sector.[3] Following the coup, the moratorium was lifted, and Canadian companies pounced on the new business opportunities.

A week after the coup, Zelaya tried to return to Honduras along with three Latin American heads of state. The military blocked his plane from landing and kept 100,000 plus supporters at bay. In doing so, the military killed two protesters and wounded at least 30. On *CTV*, Kent blamed Zelaya for the violence.[4]

Just before the elected president tried to fly into Tegucigalpa, Kent told the OAS the "time is not right" for a return, prompting Zelaya to respond dryly: "I could delay until January 27 [2010]," when his term ended.[5] Two weeks after trying the air route, Zelaya attempted to cross into Honduras by land from Nicaragua. Kent once again criticized this move. "Canada's Kent Says Zelaya Should Wait Before Return to Honduras," read a July 20 *Bloomberg* headline. A July 25 right-wing Honduran newspaper blared: "Canadá pide a Zelaya no entrar al país hasta llegar a un acuerdo" (Canada asks Zelaya not to enter the country until there's a negotiated solution).[6]

Despite the coup and the repression that followed, Ottawa refused to exclude Honduras from its Military Training Assistance Program. Though only five Honduran troops were being trained in Canada, failing to suspend relations with a military responsible for overthrowing an elected government was highly symbolic. More significantly, Canada was the only major donor to Honduras—the largest recipient of Canadian assistance in Central America—that failed to sever any aid to the military government. The World Bank, European Union, and even the US suspended some of their planned assistance to Honduras.

In response to the conflicting signals from North American leaders, the ousted Honduran foreign minister told *Telesur* that Ottawa and Washington were providing "oxygen" to the military government.[7] Patricia Rodas called on Canada and the US to suspend aid to the de facto regime. During an official visit to Mexico with Zelaya, Rodas asked Mexican president Felipe Calderón, who was about to meet Harper and President Obama, to lobby Ottawa and Washington on their behalf. "We are asking [Calderón] to be an intermediary for our people with the powerful countries of the world," said Rodas, "for example, the US and at this moment Canada, which have lines of military and economic support with Honduras."[8]

Five months after Zelaya was ousted, the coup government held previously scheduled elections. During the campaign period, the de facto government imposed martial law and censored media outlets. Dozens of candidates withdrew from local and national races and opposition presidential candidate, Carlos H. Reyes, was hospitalized following a severe beating from security forces. A protest in Tegucigalpa on election-day was forcefully repressed. Hondurans voted in "a climate of harassment, violence, and violation of the rights to freedom of expression, association and assembly," according to the Washington-based Center for Justice and International Law.[9]

The November 2009 election was boycotted by the UN and OAS and most Hondurans abstained from the poll. Despite mandatory voting regulations, only 45% of those eligible cast a ballot (it may have been much lower as this was the government's accounting). Ottawa endorsed this electoral farce. "Canada congratulates the Honduran people for the relatively peaceful and orderly manner in which the country's elections were conducted," noted an official statement.[10] Peter Kent went further boldly proclaiming, "there was a strong turnout for the elections, that they appear to have been run freely and fairly, and that there was no major violence."

While most countries in the region continued to shun post-coup Honduras, Ottawa immediately recognized Porfirio Lobo after he was inaugurated as Honduran president on January 27, 2010. Kent stated, "Canada congratulates President Lobo as he begins his term. I am confident that he will provide the strong political leadership needed to help Honduras move beyond its lengthy political impasse."[11] Kent said that Lobo's election constituted "the beginning of a process of renewal." He remained silent on the growing number of assassinations of prominent social activists, including LGBTQ rights activist Walter Tróchez, who was kidnapped, beaten, and murdered by men in police uniforms just a few weeks before the inauguration.

Ottawa supported Honduras' re-entry into the OAS, which was opposed by most member states. During a March 2012 visit, Canada's minister of state Diane Ablonczy called Honduras an "important" partner in the Americas.

Overall, the Canada-backed coup sparked a major upsurge in grassroots political activism. Hondurans mobilized in support of Zelaya and against the illegitimate government. Protestors also called for more fundamental reforms to their highly unequal society, beginning with a constituent assembly to rewrite the country's constitution.

The de-facto government and elite sectors responded with repression. Amnesty International described "the damage to human rights protection and the rule of law that followed the 2009 coup." In the two years after Zelaya's overthrow, hundreds were killed in political violence and many more attacked or injured. In May 2012

Reporters Without Borders noted, "His [Erick Avila's] death brings to 19 the number of journalists who were supporters of former president Manuel Zelaya, who have been killed since his overthrow in a coup three years ago next month." None of the murders had been solved.

Ottawa stayed silent on the detention, torture, and murder of anti-coup activists. During an August 2011 visit to Honduras, Harper said Canada had "no information to suggest that [human rights abuses] are in any way perpetrated by the government." Deciding this wasn't a sufficient endorsement of the regime's human rights record, the prime minister called Lobo "a prominent human rights leader in this country." Prior to his role in state-backed repression and his victory in a dubious presidential election, Lobo attended business school in Miami, oversaw his wealthy family's cattle ranches and was a member of Congress who insisted on reintroducing the death penalty.

During the prime minister's visit, the two countries signed a free trade accord. In the midst of significant state-backed repression, the Conservatives gave the regime a boost of legitimacy by commencing bilateral trade negotiations with the Lobo administration in October 2010. Before the coup, Ottawa was negotiating a joint Central American trade accord with Honduras, Guatemala, El Salvador, and Nicaragua, but the Conservatives dropped these plans when they found Lobo more accepting of their conditions.

Ottawa's hostility towards Zelaya was likely motivated by particular corporate interests, not only in the mining sector, but also in textile manufacturing. Zelaya's move to raise the minimum wage by 60% at the start of 2009 could not have gone down well with the Montréal-based Gildan, one of the world's biggest blank T-shirt makers. Gildan's plants had previously been based in Montréal, but the company moved its manufacturing centres to Honduras because of its low wages and poor labour regulations (in Montréal, by contrast, Gildan workers were unionized). At the time of the coup, Gildan, which met regularly with Foreign Affairs officials and Canadian politicians, produced about half of its garments in Honduras. Gildan employed more than 11,000 Hondurans and the country figured prominently in the company's growth strategy.

. Under pressure from the US-based Maquila Solidarity Network, Nike, Gap, and another US-based apparel company operating in Honduras called for the restoration of democracy two weeks after Zelaya was overthrown. Gildan refused to sign this statement. Without a high-profile brand name, Gildan was particularly dependent on producing apparel at the lowest cost possible and was presumably antagonistic towards Zelaya's move to increase the minimum wage.

During his August 2011 trip, Harper visited a Gildan facility located in a northern Honduras export processing zone where foreign companies were exempt from taxes as well as standard labour and environmental regulations. "As a general rule, our Canadian companies have a very good record of social responsibility,"

Harper told reporters on a tour of the facility. "[Gildan] pays above minimum wage. It runs health, nutrition and transport programs for its employees and is a very good corporate citizen." While the prime minister sung the company's praise, demonstrators carried banners criticizing Gildan's labour practices and Harper's support for the coup. Some Gildan workers tried to deliver an open letter to the prime minister drafted by the Honduran Women's Collective.

The mining sector was another beneficiary of the coup. In addition to the mining moratorium, Zelaya had also responded to grassroots pressure by drafting a new mining code that called for greater community consent for mining projects, an end to open-pit mining and the use of cyanide in new concessions. It also increased royalty rates. The coup interrupted the final reading of the proposed mining law.

Rights Action uncovered credible information that a subsidiary of Vancouver-based Goldcorp, the world's second biggest gold producer, provided money to those who rallied in support of the coup:

> On a number of occasions, mine workers, ex-mine workers and other local young men, have travelled in buses from the Siria Valley to Tegucigalpa to participate in pro-coup marches organized by the pro-coup Movement for Peace and Democracy that is funded by the Honduran private sector ... The buses from the Siria Valley are contracted to Entremares [Goldcorp's wholly owned subsidiary]; These bus trips are coordinated by local men who work or used to work with Entremares; who work or used to work as 'community promoters'

with the Fundacion San Martin (a local NGO set up and funded by Entremares); and who work with the Honduran Association of Mining, that Entremares is a member of ... The men and young men are contacted one by one, and asked if they would like to go on the bus, for 400 Lempiras (over US$20). If they agree, they are told to meet at such and such a point, in the Siria Valley, and the bus picks them up in the morning ... When the bus gets to the protest, in Tegucigalpa, they are wearing their white t-shirts [the colour of the coup supporters]. They are told to stay in the area of the protest, and to meet back at the bus at 3pm. They were told to shout along with the pro-democracy and pro-peace slogans of the pro-coup rally organizers.

Soon after Lobo took office, Canadian government and mining officials began pressing the president to pass a new mining law. The English language *Honduras Weekly* reported on a February 2010 meeting between the president and Canadian ambassador Neil Reeder:

President Porfirio Lobo met Tuesday with Canada's ambassador to Honduras, Neil Reeder, and a group of Canadian businessmen, including the president of Aura Minerals, Inc., Patrick Downey, and investor David Petroff ... Ambassador Reeder expressed his interest in expanding Canada's investments in the Honduran mining and maquila sectors. He specifically mentioned the need to establish new mining regulations that would both protect the interests of foreign mining companies in Honduras and create transparency in mining operations. Mr. Reeder estimated potential investments in Honduras of up to US$700 million and pointed out the benefits to the country in terms of jobs creation and additional tax revenues. Mining in Honduras by foreign multinationals has traditionally been a source of contention, with one side arguing in favor of business interests and another pointing out the environmental damages caused by open pit mining and the use of chemicals such as cyanide.

The Honduran right-wing retained power for twelve years after the coup, relying on state repression, North American support, and rigged elections that first brought to power Porfirio Lobo (2010-2014) and later Juan Orlando Hernández (2014-2022).

PARAGUAY, 2012

In 2012, the left-leaning president of Paraguay, Fernando Lugo, was ousted in what some called an "institutional coup." Upset with Lugo for disrupting sixty-one years of one-party rule by the conservative Colorado Party, Paraguay's traditional ruling elite claimed he was responsible for a murky incident that left seventeen peasants and police dead and the senate voted to impeach the president.

On June 15, 2012, 300 police officers descended on the town of Curuguaty to evict 70 landless farmers from their property. The land was state owned before military dictator Alfredo Stroessner, who ruled from 1954-1989, transferred ownership to a friend. The confrontation, whose exact details remain muddled, led to the death of eleven campesinos and six policemen. Right-wing forces in Congress used the killings as a pretext to impeach President Lugo, accusing the former bishop of aligning with the farmers.

The vast majority of countries in the hemisphere refused to recognize the new government. The Union of South American Nations (UNASUR) suspended Paraguay's membership after Lugo's ouster, as did the MERCOSUR trading bloc. "Not a single Latin American government has recognized [Federico] Franco's presidency," reported the Council on Hemispheric Affairs.

But Canada was one of only a handful of countries in the world that immediately recognized the new government. "Canada notes that Fernando Lugo has accepted the decision of the Paraguayan Senate to impeach him and that a new president, Federico Franco, has been sworn in," said Diane Ablonczy, minister of state for foreign affairs, the day after the coup. This statement was premature. After a confusing initial statement, Lugo rejected his ouster and announced the creation of a parallel government.

Lugo's reformist program was a thorn in the side of the conservative establishment and powerful agribusiness. Paraguay is largely reliant on agricultural exports, particularly soy. But, growing soy production, which requires large amounts of land, intensified displacement and the growth of landless farmers.

Lugo's agrarian populism and position as a political outsider struck a chord with the imperiled campesino population. But the state apparatus established during the long Colorado party rule prevented the "bishop of the poor's" attempts at reform. Lugo's struggle to impose a five-percent tax on soy exports was suppressed and powerful farming corporations launched protests that forced him to reverse an executive order to limit the use of pesticides.

The swift politicization of the Curuguaty massacre by the right-wing establishment, coupled with numerous discrepancies in the official investigation and the murder of a key peasant witness shortly before testifying, led many progressives to believe the incident may have been manufactured to remove the would-be reformist from the presidency. Whether or not this is true, the judiciary immediately blamed the peasants for the incident and persecuted them at the expense of an open inquiry into the police's actions. The coup was integral to returning the Colorado Party, which expanded rules on genetically modified seeds, rejected calls to raise taxes on soy exports and accelerated agricultural consolidation.

A week after the coup against Lugo, Ottawa participated in an Organization of American States (OAS) mission that many member countries opposed. Largely designed to undermine the countries calling for Paraguay's suspension from the OAS, delegates from the US, Canada, Haiti, Honduras, and Mexico travelled to Paraguay to investigate Lugo's removal from office. Minister of state of foreign affairs Diane Ablonczy said the aim of the OAS mission was to "provide important context from Paraguay to inform international reaction. It is important that we avoid a rush to judgment and focus on the best interests of the Paraguayan people." The delegation concluded that the OAS should not suspend Paraguay, which displeased many South American countries.

In an interview three weeks after his ouster, Lugo alluded to Ottawa's hostility toward Paraguay's efforts at regional cooperation with other Latin American states. "With the current polarization between the United States, Canada, and Mexico on one end and South America on the other, we have tried to find regional alternatives. The coup d'état now attempts to attack the [South American] regional integration efforts." Both the Canadian Labour Congress and the newly formed international labour federation IndustriALL Global Union criticized the Conservatives move to recognize the new government.

In addition to agricultural exports, Paraguay relies on the mining sector, in which Canadian companies have some noteworthy investments. On a couple of occasions, the overthrown president claimed Canadian economic interests in this industry contributed to the coup. "Those who pushed for the coup are those who want to solidify the negotiations with the multinational Rio Tinto Alcan, betraying the energetic sovereignty and interests of our country," Lugo told his supporters one month after the coup. IndustriALL Global Union concurred with the president, sending a letter to the CEO of Rio Tinto. "Rio Tinto, which has a legendary association with the government of Canada, has been quick off the mark to resume negotiations on behalf of Montréal-based Rio Tinto Alcan for a $4 billion aluminum plant," wrote Jyrki Raina, general secretary of IndustriALL Global Union. The labour federation called on "Rio Tinto to publicly disclose its interest and involvement, if any, in the coup d'état in Paraguay and the ousting of a legitimately elected democratic government of Fernando Lugo."

In 2010, Montréal-based Rio Tinto Alcan, a subsidiary of Rio Tinto, began lobbying the Paraguayan government for subsidized electricity to set up a massive aluminum plant near the Paraná River. The company was seeking a thirty-year contract that could cost Paraguay's government hundreds of millions of dollars and they received Ottawa's backing. According to international media reports, the Canadian Embassy in Buenos Aires, which is in charge of the country's diplomatic relations in Paraguay, lobbied the government on Rio Tinto Alcan's behalf. The Lugo government was divided over the project, which would consume more energy than the country's entire 6.5 million population and damage the environment in various other ways. Three weeks before Lugo's ouster vice president Federico Franco, who represented an opposition party, complained to *Ultima Hora* newspaper: "I told the President of the Republic (Lugo): why did you send me to Canada to study the [aluminum] project if, finally, a Deputy Minister (Mercedes Canese) was going to oppose it."

After the coup, the vice president became president and announced that negotiations with Rio Tinto Alcan would be fast tracked. Since then, neoliberalism and Colorado Party domination have remained steadfast in Paraguay.

UKRAINE, 2014

Between 2010 and 2014, Canada waged a campaign to subvert a Ukrainian president who won elections the Organization for Security and Co-operation in Europe called "an impressive display of democracy."[1] This electoral interference played out in a context of intense and sometimes violent rivalry between two political camps, one in Ukraine's west aligned with Western Europe and North America, and another in Ukraine's east, which leaned towards Russia.

The 2010 Ukrainian presidential election and 2012 parliamentary elections were won by Viktor Yanukovych and his Party of Regions. His victory was due to votes from the largely Russian-speaking regions in the east and south of Ukraine. Ottawa sent observers to monitor these elections. Following his victory, Yanukovych passed legislation codifying Ukrainian neutrality in the geopolitical confrontation between NATO and Russia, which increasingly played out in Ukraine. This move was not welcomed by Ottawa, a staunch proponent of expanding NATO eastward, including into Ukraine.

Ottawa has sought to destabilize the relationship between Russia and Ukraine since the early days of the USSR. In 1940, for example, the federal government helped establish the nationalist and anti-Soviet

Ukrainian Canadian Congress. In 1952, External Affairs launched a Ukrainian section of Radio Canada International to disseminate an anti-Soviet perspective. Additionally, Canada accepted thousands of Ukrainian Nazi collaborators who fled Europe after World War II.[2] The right-wing historical narrative passed down for generations by some of these diaspora groups is evidenced by numerous monuments glorifying Nazi collaborators, including a cenotaph honouring the Ukrainian Galician Division of the Waffen-SS in the St. Volodymyr Ukrainian Cemetery in Oakville, Ontario.

The affinity between the Canadian state and Ukrainian nationalists persisted well into the twenty-first century. One of the most well-known examples of this alliance can be found in the personal history of deputy prime minister Chrystia Freeland, whose grandfather Mykhailo Chomiak was a Ukrainian Nazi propagandist during WWII. Chomiak operated a pro-Nazi newspaper from an apartment that had belonged to Jews sent to concentration camps. After the war, he emigrated to Canada and, alongside his granddaughter Chrystia, worked on *The Encyclopedia of Ukraine*, an academic project "which touted a hardline, far-right, and anti-Soviet position in its historical narrative."[3]

Yanukovych sought a middle ground between Russia and the West. In response, Ottawa immediately worked to undermine his government. Months after Yanukovych became president, Prime Minister Harper declared, "there are issues that are of concern to Ukrainian-Canadians and to the government of Canada involving issues of human rights and the rule of law, and I'll be raising those with President Yanukovych."[4] Ukrainian Canadian Congress (UCC) head Paul Grod and other representatives of the ultra-nationalist organization accompanied the prime minister during his October 2010 visit to Ukraine. In announcing their participation, the UCC release claimed, "recent steps taken by Ukraine's political leadership have seriously undermined the country's constitution, its democratic institutions, the protection of its historical memory and national identity, sovereignty and territorial integrity."[5]

During the trip, Stephen Harper met opposition leaders, including failed presidential candidate Yulia Tymoshenko. In Lviv, Harper visited a controversial new nationalist museum and met its director, who had recently been accused of passing classified information to third parties. Talking to journalists about Ukraine's 1932 famine, Harper encouraged the public to challenge their government, saying the famine should "remind the Ukrainian people of the importance of their freedom and democracy and independence, and of the necessity of always defending those things."[6] With Yanukovych refusing to echo Harper's nationalist interpretation of the 1932 famine, Lubomyr Luciuk, a Royal Military College of Canada professor who participated in Harper's tour, wrote in the *Kingston Whig-Standard*, "Yanukovych is slated for the dustbin of history while the honourable Harper can stand proud."

A year after his trip, Harper threatened Yanukovych over legal proceedings against Tymoshenko, who was found guilty of corruption. In an October 2011 letter, Canada's PM wrote, "I cannot overstate the potential negative impact of the current judicial proceedings against Yulia Tymoshenko on both Ukraine's future relations with Canada and others and on Ukraine's long-term democratic development."[7] During an April 2012 visit, international trade minister Beverly Oda said Canada was deeply concerned about human rights abuses and, in a highly abnormal diplomatic move, had Ukrainian-Canadian representatives participating in her delegation criticize the government. One need only imagine a Russian delegation bringing Russian-Canadians, or a Chinese delegation bringing Chinese-Canadians, to criticize Ottawa to understand the peculiarity of this decision.

In a bid to heighten political tensions and subvert parliamentary elections, Harper attacked Yanukovych in front of a large group of Canadians about to monitor that country's vote. In October 2012 the PM declared, "we continue to call upon President Yanukovych to respect judicial independence, to cease the harassment of opposition voices, and to conduct an election that is indeed free and fair."[8] Harper pressed the monitors to raise their voice, stating, "never forget, that the vigilant watcher can hold rulers to account, that the one who sees and speaks up is truly the guardian of liberty."

Further encouraging opposition to the government, citizenship, immigration and multiculturalism minister Jason Kenney announced funding for a project "to strengthen freedom of expression, freedom of information and free media in Ukraine."[9] Launched during a March 2013 visit, the initiative was designed to boost antigovernment forces.

Ottawa helped encourage the Maidan protests by breathlessly criticizing the Yanukovych government. It is quite clear that if Yanukovych's main competitor in the 2010 election, Yulia Tymoshenko, had won and committed five times more rights violations, she would have received far less criticism.

The overthrow of Yanukovych in the 2014 Maidan protests, which led to his unconstitutional replacement by a Washington-selected government, amounted to what Guardian columnist Seumas Milne called "the imposition of a pro-western government on Russia's most neuralgic and politically divided neighbour."[10] The effects of this intervention, Milne predicted in April 2014, would be catastrophic: "The US and EU have already overplayed their hand in Ukraine. Neither Russia nor the western powers may want to intervene directly... [b]ut a century after 1914, the risk of unintended consequences should be obvious enough— as the threat of a return of big-power conflict grows. Pressure for a negotiated end to the crisis is essential."[11]

Ottawa and the Ukrainian Canadian Congress began assisting nationalist, anti-Russian, Ukrainians prior to the USSR's breakup in 1991.[12] Through the 1990s, Canada played an outsized role in shaping the newly independent nation's politics. Canada was the first country after Poland to recognize Ukraine's independence and the first western country to offer credit. Canadians helped draft the country's inaugural constitution and many Canadian advisers, generally from the Ukrainian community, were assigned to positions within Ukrainian ministries and agencies. Even the currency used after independence was printed in Canada.

In the lead up to the 2004 Orange Revolution, Canada funnelled hundreds of thousands of dollars to the groups that protested against a close presidential election in which Yanukovych was initially declared victor. The lead group behind the organization of the Orange Revolution, Pora, received US$30,000 from the Canadian Embassy, which was its first donation. Canadian ambassador Andrew Robinson, reported the *Globe and Mail*, "organized secret monthly meetings of western ambassadors" to support Yanukovych's rival Viktor Yushchenko. The 2004 protests and subsequent election redo deepened the country's geographical and linguistic divisions.

In the two decades before the Maidan uprising, Canada channelled tens, probably hundreds, of millions of dollars to anti-Russian elements of Ukrainian civil society.[13] During a July 2007 visit to Ukraine, foreign affairs minister Peter MacKay announced $16 million in assistance for democratic reform to "counter-balance" Russia. "There are outside pressures, from Russia most notably," noted MacKay. "We want to make sure they feel the support that is there for them in the international community." In 2013, US assistant secretary of state Victoria Nuland boasted that the National Endowment for Democracy (NED), USAID, and other US government agencies had plowed $5 billion into bolstering Western-oriented forces in Ukraine since 1991.[14] In a sign of Ottawa's close ties to opposition activists, throughout the Maidan protests the Canadian Embassy's local spokesperson, Inna Tsarkova, was a prominent member of AutoMaidan, an anti-government group that organized protests in front of Yanukovych's residence calling for the president to go.[15] As the embassy's Program Officer, Tsarkova had previously led sessions about acquiring Canadian funding.[16] Two months into the Maidan protests, Tsarkova's car was set ablaze. In an interview with a Ukrainian Canadian radio program two days after the long-time employee at the Canadian Embassy said, "if we don't stand up enough then you know it means the end of Ukraine in terms of democracy and real freedoms. It will be the Soviet empire back in the 1930s when people were just thrown into prison and killed."[17]

The Maidan protests were sparked by Yanukovych stalling on the European Union–Ukraine Association Agreement. The free trade accord was a step forward in the process of the country potentially joining the EU, which was attractive to many Ukrainians, especially in the west and centre of the country. However, the agreement was more divisive than portrayed by Canadian media and officials. Ukraine, with the second largest landmass in Europe, has significant geographical divisions. For instance, Lviv in the west is closer to Prague, Vienna and Berlin than to the eastern Ukrainian city of Kharkiv, which is near Russia. Additionally, eastern and southern Ukraine was part of the Russian empire for two centuries, while modern Ukraine's west was once part of the Polish-Lithuanian and Austro-Hungarian empires and was known as Galicia.

Joining the EU was viewed favourably by many Ukrainians, but the Association Agreement had costs as well. The EU deal would not only undercut trade with Russia; it also depended on Kyiv agreeing to the International Monetary Fund's demand for "extremely harsh conditions" on eliminating energy subsidies and other government supports.[18]

Amidst the negotiations over the Association Agreement, Moscow offered some $10 billion in benefits to Ukraine and called for tripartite (EU, Russia, and Ukraine) negotiations to work out various trade and economic issues. The EU rejected negotiations. The president of the European Commission, José Manuel Barroso, said explicitly that Kyiv had to choose between the EU Association Agreement and a customs union with Russia. The EU's take-it-or-leave-it position exacerbated deep geographical and linguistic divisions within Ukraine.

When the anti-Yanukovych uprisings began in late 2013, Canada supported the three-month-long protests. The Canadian government assisted pro-EU, including many far-right, protesters who rallied in central Kyiv's

Maidan square from November 21, 2013, to February 22, 2014. During the uprising Canada's foreign minister attended an anti-government rally and protesters used the Canadian Embassy as a safe haven for numerous days.

A little over a week into the protests, Canada released a statement critical of government repression, which University of Ottawa professor Ivan Katchanovski says was precipitated by far-right infiltrators.[19] In a November 30, 2013 release titled "Canada Condemns Use of Force Against Protesters in Ukraine," foreign affairs minister John Baird declared, "Canada strongly condemns the deplorable use of force today by Ukrainian authorities against peaceful protesters."[20] Six days later, Baird visited Maidan square with Paul Grod, president of the ultranationalist UCC.[21] From the stage, Grod announced Baird's presence and support for the protesters, which led many to chant "Thank you Canada." In recognition of Canada's important role, a Canadian flag flew at the Maidan protest.[22] Baird also called on Ukrainian authorities to respect the protests and bemoaned "the shadow that Russia is casting over this country."[23]

On December 27, Canada's chargé d'affaires visited protest leader and journalist Tetiana Chornovol in the hospital after she was violently attacked.[24] Three weeks earlier, Chornovol was widely reported to have participated in seizing Kyiv City Hall.[25] A former member of a far-right party, Chornovol had previously been arrested on numerous occasions and was subsequently charged with murder for throwing a Molotov cocktail at the Party of Regions headquarters during the Maidan protests.

Prime Minister Harper repeatedly expressed support for the protesters and criticized Yanukovych. On January 27, he slammed the Ukrainian president for "not moving towards a free and democratic Euro-Atlantic future but very much towards an anti-democratic Soviet past."[26] The next day Ottawa announced travel restrictions and economic sanctions on individuals close to the elected president. At the press conference to announce the measures, citizenship and immigration minister Chris Alexander said, "you [Yanukovych] are not welcome in Canada and we will continue to take strong action until the violence against the people of Ukraine has stopped and democracy has been restored."[27] Ottawa subsequently slapped travel bans and economic sanctions on dozens of individuals aligned with Yanukovych.

At the height of the protests, activists used the Canadian Embassy, which was immediately adjacent to Maidan square, as a safe haven for "at least a week." The protesters gained access to a mini-van and other Canadian material. In a story written a year after the coup, the Canadian Press quoted officials from allied European nations accusing Canada of being "an active participant in regime change." In his investigation of Maidan activists' use of the Canadian Embassy in Kyiv, Canadian Press reporter Murray Brewster writes, "Canadians are not very popular in some quarters and occasionally loathed by pro-Russian Ukrainians."

At least some of those allowed to use the Canadian Embassy were from the far right. In "The far right, the Euromaidan, and the Maidan massacre in Ukraine," professor Katchanovski reported, "the leader of the [far right] Svoboda-affiliated C14 admitted that his C14-based Maidan Self-Defense company took refuge in the Canadian Embassy in Kyiv on February 18 and stayed there during the Maidan massacre."[28]

On February 19 and 20, more than 50 were killed in violence that was widely blamed on government security forces. However, work by Katchanovski, BBC and others show that far-right activists were likely responsible for many of these deaths.[29]

The killings precipitated the collapse of the government. As revealed in a leaked phone call between US assistant secretary of state Victoria Nuland and ambassador to Ukraine Geoffrey Pyatt, US officials midwifed Yanukovych's unconstitutional replacement.[30] During the call the US officials decide that Arseniy Yatsenyuk, who advocated joining NATO, should take power.

After Yanukovych was ousted, Ottawa sought to shore up the unconstitutional government. Soon after, Baird "welcomed the appointment of a new government," saying, "the appointment of a legitimate government is a vital step forward in restoring democracy and normalcy to Ukraine."[31] But the country's constitutional provisions dealing with replacing or impeaching a president were flagrantly violated. While Ukraine's

Parliament passed a resolution backing Yanukovych's ouster, the impeachment procedure enshrined in Article 111 of the constitution requires a special investigatory commission to formulate charges against the president, a ruling by the Constitutional Court and Supreme Court and multiple (decisive) votes in parliament.[32]

Days after the coup, Baird led a delegation of Conservative Party MPs and Ukrainian-Canadian representatives to meet acting president Oleksandr Turchynov and new prime minister Arseniy Yatsenyuk, who was Nuland's preference.[33] Canada's foreign minister announced an immediate $200,000 in medical assistance for those injured in the political violence.[34] Subsequently, Ottawa announced $220 million in aid to the interim government.[35] Harper said, "I think we really have to credit the Ukrainian people themselves with resisting the attempt to overturn their democracy and to lead their country back into the past."[36]

After the coup, Canada's PM was the first G7 leader to visit the interim government.[37] Alongside Baird and justice minister Peter MacKay, Harper told the acting president, "you have provided inspiration and a new chapter in humanity's ongoing story of the struggle for freedom, democracy and justice."[38] During his visit to shore up the US and Canadian-installed government, Harper accused Vladimir Putin of seeking to destabilize international security and return the world to the "law of the jungle." In support of the unconstitutional change of power, Harper visited the authorities in Kyiv twice in under two months.

The individual who became president three months after the Maidan protests said, "Canada is one of Ukraine's closest partners." During his September 2014 visit to Ottawa, Petro Poroshenko added that Ukraine had "no better friend."

The post-Yanukovych government banned a number of major political parties and empowered far-right forces that perpetrated significant violence, including a massacre of at least 42 individuals at the headquarters of the Odessa federation of trade unions. Ottawa stayed quiet about the massacre in Odessa and the ban on opposition parties.

The 2014 coup divided Ukraine politically, geographically, and linguistically. The largely Russian-speaking south and east protested the ouster of Yanukovych, who was from the region. Likewise, many opposed the post-coup right-wing nationalist government because it immediately eliminated Russian as an official language and prohibited education in Russian, Polish, and Hungarian (Magyar) while making moves to rehabilitate hardline anti-Soviet historical figures, including Nazi collaborators, by building statues and renaming streets.

The 2014 coup prompted Moscow to seize Crimea with its largely Russian population and strategically important Russian naval base. Additionally, the coup and the subsequent violence against Russian speakers, including the Odessa massacre, prompted thousands of Ukrainians in the eastern Donbass region to rebel against the new Western-backed government in Kyiv.

Moscow offered this endogenous uprising military and logistical support. The Donbass then became the site of an eight-year war that left 14,000 people dead and contributed to Russia's 2022 invasion of Ukraine.

BRAZIL, 2016

In 2016, Brazilian Workers' Party president Dilma Rousseff was impeached through a "soft coup." A little more than a year into her second four-year term, parliamentarians voted Rousseff out, having found her guilty of breaking Brazil's budget laws. The impeachment was sparked by an economic downturn and the massive *Lava Jato* corruption probe that targeted various politicians, including her Workers' Party predecessor, Lula da Silva. There was no evidence of Rousseff's corruption and the case against former president, Lula da Silva, was flimsy at best. The lead prosecutor, who under the Brazilian system also acts as a judge, Sergio Moro, later became justice minister in the Jair Bolsonaro government.

In mid-2019, *The Intercept* released a trove of communications from Moro, confirming the political nature of the charges against Lula, which had the effect of weakening Rousseff due to her association with the former president.[1] The documents also revealed that prosecutors worked with US authorities during the investigation, sometimes keeping their cooperation secret from the Rousseff administration.[2] There are frequent references to the FBI in the leaked conversations, which clearly communicate that "the closest relationship [was] between members of the Brazilian PF [Federal Police] and the FBI agents."

While the Trudeau government made dozens of statements criticizing Venezuela under Nicolás Maduro, Ottawa remained silent on Rousseff's ouster and persecution of the left in Brazil. The only comment we found was a Global Affairs official telling Sputnik that Canada would maintain relations with Brazil after Rousseff was impeached.[3] Soon after, Canada began negotiating to join the Brazilian led MERCOSUR trade bloc (just after Venezuela was expelled).[4] They also held a Canada Brazil Strategic Dialogue Partnership.[5]

In October 2018, Global Affairs minister Chrystia Freeland met her Brazilian counterpart to discuss, among other issues, pressuring the Venezuelan government. She tweeted, "Canada and Brazil enjoy a strong friendship and we are thankful for your support in defending the international rules-based order and holding the Maduro regime in Venezuela to account." After Rousseff's ouster, Brazil joined the anti-Maduro Lima Group that Canada helped create.

In 2018, the openly sexist, racist, anti-environmental politician Jair Bolsonaro won the presidential election largely because the front runner in the polls had been jailed on dubious charges. Former Workers' Party president Lula da Silva, who ended his second term with an 83% approval rating due to largely successful policies aimed at alleviating extreme hunger and growing Brazil's GDP, was blocked from running due to these politically motivated corruption charges.[6] The Trudeau government was publicly silent on Lula's imprisonment. The night before the Supreme Court was set to determine Lula's fate, the general in charge of the army hinted at military intervention if the judges ruled in favour of the popular former president.[7] Not even that outrageous statement was criticized by Ottawa.

At the G20 meeting in June 2019, Trudeau warmly welcomed Bolsonaro and Canada continued negotiating the Canada-Mercosur Free Trade Agreement with the new right-wing government.[8] In August 2019, NDP leader Jagmeet Singh called on Trudeau to halt negotiations with MERCOSUR due to the intensification of deforestation under Bolsonaro. Nevertheless, the Trudeau government continued to negotiate an agreement with Bolsonaro's Brazil. Furthermore, Ottawa made no comment when Bolsonaro was twice reported to the International Criminal Court for "incitement to genocide" against the Indigenous peoples living on protected lands.

With over $10 billion invested in Brazil, corporate Canada appeared excited by the prospects of a right-wing president.[9] After his election, CBC reported, "for Canadian business, a Bolsonaro presidency could open new investment opportunities, especially in the resource sector, finance and infrastructure, as he has pledged to slash environmental regulations in the Amazon rainforest and privatize some government-owned companies."[10] Ottawa's quiet support for the 2016 "soft coup" in Brazil mirrored Canada's backing of the 1964 military coup against president João Goulart. Both were partially motivated by corporate interests and saw the rise of right-wing reactionaries.

BOLIVIA, 2019

In November 2019, Ottawa supported the ouster of Bolivian president Evo Morales. During that period, an alliance of economic elites, Christian extremists, and security forces backed by Washington deposed Morales, Bolivia's first Indigenous president, and replaced him with an unconstitutional government led by rightist Jeanine Áñez, whose party won 4% of the vote in the 2019 elections.[1] The unconstitutional post-coup government immediately attacked Indigenous symbols and authorized massacres of pro-democracy protestors in the cities of Sacaba and Senkata, killing 32.[2] Hundreds were arrested in political repression with many journalists detained and media outlets such as *Telesur, RT en Español*, and dozens of local and community-based radio stations shuttered.[3] Meanwhile, many MAS officials fled Bolivia in fear for their lives as the armed forces committed repeated acts of violence against members and supporters of Morales' political party.

Prior to his removal in the November 2019 coup, Evo Morales had been president of Bolivia for thirteen years. He won four presidential elections as head of the left-wing Movement for Socialism (MAS), a political party founded by coca farmers. As the party's long-serving leader, Morales became the figurehead of a grassroots Indigenous-led fight against neoliberalism and imperialism in the only country in South America where the majority of the population identifies as Indigenous.

Deep-seated racist attitudes amongst the country's middle-to-upper class white population played a substantial role in opposition to MAS rule.[4] The racist character of the new regime became obvious after Morales was overthrown in November 2019. Luis Fernando Camacho, an extreme right-wing politician from the affluent Santa Cruz department, declared that Pachamama, a goddess revered by the Indigenous Andean peoples of South America, "will never return to the [presidential] palace. Bolivia belongs to Christ."[5] The new opposition government then tore the Indigenous *Wiphala* flag from government buildings. After proclaiming herself interim president, the unelected Áñez carried a large Bible into the presidential palace and declared, "Thank god, the Bible has returned to the Bolivian government." Such behaviour is hardly surprising given that in 2013 Áñez tweeted, "I dream of a Bolivia without satanic Indigenous rituals, the city isn't made for Indians, they need to go back to the countryside."[6]

While the Morales government's majoritarian character infuriated Bolivia's well-off white population, its foreign policy brought a chill to its relations with the US. Morales aligned Bolivia with the left-wing governments that won elections across Latin America in the early 2000s, some of which were ousted in Canadian-backed coups. Under his tenure, Bolivia joined the Venezuela-led Bolivarian Alliance for the Peoples of Our America (ALBA) and the Union of South American Nations (UNASUR), which were championed as alternatives to the US led neoliberal geopolitical order. For its part, Canada strongly supported the expansion of neoliberal policies across Latin America and aggressively lobbied for the Free Trade Area of the Americas.

Morales also increased medical cooperation with Cuba, expelled USAID from Bolivia, and cut off diplomatic ties with Israel after Israel's devastating war on Gaza in 2009. Following the coup against Morales, the "caretaker" regime of Jeanine Áñez expelled 700 Cuban doctors, returned USAID to the country, restarted diplomatic relations with Israel, and joined the anti-Venezuela Lima Group. These moves were made during what should have been the two final months of Morales' 2015 election mandate, which no one seriously disputed. As unelected president, Áñez also fired 80% of MAS-appointed ambassadors and took out a US$327 million loan from the IMF while completely failing to contain the COVID-19 pandemic.

The pretext for Morales' overthrow in 2019 was the claim that the October 20 presidential election was flawed. Few disputed that Morales won the first round, but some claimed that he did not reach the 10% margin of victory, which was the threshold required to avoid a second-round runoff. The official result was 47.1% for Morales and 36.5% for right-wing US-backed candidate Carlos Mesa.

Hours after the military command forced Morales to resign as president of the most Indigenous nation in the Americas, Chrystia Freeland endorsed the coup. The foreign minister released a statement noting, "Canada stands with Bolivia and the democratic will of its people. We note the resignation of President Morales and will continue to support Bolivia during this transition and the new elections."[7] Freeland's statement had no hint of criticism of Morales' ouster while leaders from Argentina to Cuba and Venezuela to Mexico condemned Morales' forced resignation.

Ten days earlier, Global Affairs bolstered right-wing anti-Morales protests by echoing the Trump administration's criticism of Morales' first round election victory. "It is not possible to accept the outcome under these circumstances," said a Global Affairs statement.[8] "We join our international partners in calling for a second round of elections to restore credibility in the electoral process."[9]

At the same time, Justin Trudeau raised concerns about Bolivia's election with other leaders. During a phone conversation with Chilean president Sebastián Piñera, the prime minister criticized "election irregularities in Bolivia."[10] Ottawa also promoted and financed the OAS' effort to discredit Bolivia's presidential election.

After the October 20 presidential poll, the OAS immediately cried foul. The next day, the organization released a statement expressing "its deep concern and surprise at the drastic and hard-to-explain change in the trend of the preliminary results [from the quick count] revealed after the closing of the polls." Two days later they followed that statement up with a preliminary report that repeated their claim that "changes in the TREP [quick count] trend were hard to explain and did not match the other measurements available."

The "hard-to-explain" changes cited by the OAS were entirely expected, as detailed in the Washington-based Center for Economic Policy Research's report "What Happened in Bolivia's 2019 Vote Count? The Role of the OAS Electoral Observation Mission." The CEPR analysis pointed out that Morales' percentage lead over the second-place candidate Carlos Mesa increased steadily as votes from rural, largely Indigenous, areas were tabulated. Additionally, the 47.1% of the vote Morales garnered aligned with pre-election polls and the vote score for the MAS party. The hullabaloo about the quick count stopping at 83% of the vote was preplanned and there was no evidence of a pause in the actual counting.

Subsequent investigations corroborated CEPR's analysis. A *Washington Post* commentary published by researchers at MIT's Election Data and Science Lab was titled "Bolivia dismissed its October elections as fraudulent. Our research found no reason to suspect fraud."[11] *The New York Times* reported on a study by three other US academics suggesting the OAS audit was flawed. The story noted that "a close look at Bolivian election data suggests an initial analysis by the OAS that raised questions of vote-rigging—and helped force out a president—was flawed."[12]

The OAS' statements gave oxygen to opposition protests. Their unsubstantiated criticism of the election was also widely cited internationally to justify Morales' ouster. In response to OAS claims, as well as protests in Bolivia and Washington and Ottawa saying they would not recognize Morales' victory, the Bolivian president agreed to a "binding" OAS audit of the first round of the election. Unsurprisingly the OAS' preliminary audit report alleged "irregularities and manipulation" and called for new elections overseen by a new electoral commission.

Immediately after the OAS released its preliminary audit US secretary of state Mike Pompeo went further, saying "all government officials and officials of any political organizations implicated in the flawed October 20 elections should step aside from the electoral process." [13] What started with an easy-to-explain discrepancy between the quick count and final results of the counting spiraled into rhetoric of "the entire election is suspect and anyone associated with it must go."

At a Special Meeting of the OAS Permanent Council on Bolivia, the representative of Antigua and Barbuda criticized the opaque way in which the OAS electoral mission to Bolivia released its statements and reports.[14] She pointed out how the organization made a series of agreements with the Bolivian government that were effectively jettisoned. A number of Latin American countries echoed this view. For his part, Morales said the OAS "is in the service of the North American empire."[15]

US and Canadian representatives, on the other hand, applauded the OAS' work in Bolivia. Canada's representative to the OAS boasted that two Canadian technical advisers were part of the audit mission to Bolivia and that Canada financed the OAS effort that discredited Bolivia's presidential election.[16] During this time Canada was also the second largest contributor to the OAS, which received half its budget from Washington.[17] In a statement titled "Canada welcomes results of OAS electoral audit mission to Bolivia," Freeland noted, "Canada commends the invaluable work of the OAS audit mission in ensuring a fair and transparent process, which we supported financially and through our expertise."[18]

Even after a number of academic and corporate media studies demonstrated the partisan nature of the OAS audit mission, Global Affairs continued to promote the organization's involvement in Bolivia's elections. In the lead up to the post-coup election, Global Affairs' Canada in Bolivia account tweeted, "Canada is pleased to support the Organization of American States (OAS) electoral observation mission to Bolivia."

The anti-democratic nature of Canada's position grew starker with time. After dragging their feet on elections initially set for January, the "interim" government used the COVID-19 pandemic as an excuse to repeatedly postpone elections. Global Affairs ignored the "caretaker" government's repeated postponement of elections. Even worse, when the country's social movements launched a general strike in August 2020 to protest Áñez's repeated postponement of elections, Global Affairs echoed the coup government's claims that the protests undermined the fight against the COVID-19 pandemic. Canada in Bolivia tweeted, "Canada calls for humanitarian aid to be allowed to circulate freely in Bolivia to fight COVID 19 and calls on all social actors to support the country's democratic institutions and to use those mechanisms to resolve any disputes."[19] The statement omitted the fact that protestors let ambulances and other medical vehicles circulate with little disruption.

Ottawa stayed silent while the unelected Jeanine Áñez regime ramped up political repression and anti-Indigenous measures. During her year of unelected rule, the Canada in Bolivia Twitter account did not release a single statement criticizing the coup government. Over the same period, Canada in Bolivia tweeted 15 statements critical of the Venezuelan government. Worse than silence, Global Affairs Canada claimed on Bolivia's Independence Day in August 2020 that Canada and Bolivia's "strong bilateral relationship is founded on our shared values of democracy, human rights and a celebration of diversity."[20]

The undemocratic nature of Canadian policy was confirmed with the victory by Morales' former finance minister, Luis Arce, in the October 2020 election. In a decisive rebuke of Ottawa's support for the coup, Arce won 55% of the vote for president and the MAS party took a large majority in the Congress.

On November 9, 2020—roughly one year after Canada supported the violent coup that overthrew him—Morales crossed the border from Argentina into Bolivia, marking the end of his exile. His return was greeted by enormous crowds from rural and predominantly Indigenous regions of the country.

Diplomacy

Bolivia

on the dais
a giant
bible rests

it proclaims
the end of
pagan rule

we will lend
a hand to
the oligarchs

they'll flood
the streets
with peasant

blood spark
calls for
retribution

A Poem by Rob Rolfe

PERU, 2022

On December 7, 2022, elected president Pedro Castillo was impeached and jailed. Ottawa immediately backed the removal of a president whose government called the Canadian-backed anti-Venezuela Lima Group "the most disastrous thing we have done in international politics in the history of Perú."[1]

Born to illiterate peasants in Cajamarca, one of the poorest regions in Peru, Castillo became a primary school teacher and union activist. He rose to national prominence by leading a teachers' strike in 2017. Castillo's rise was symbolically important for Indigenous, rural, and impoverished Peruvians. But it elicited contempt from the Lima elite who sought to humiliate him at every turn. Partly as a result of an unrelenting sabotage campaign, Castillo was ineffective in pursuing his agenda of lessening the country's gross inequities. Among other positions, Castillo vowed to reform the Fujimori-era constitution and implement agrarian reform to promote food security and sustainable small-scale production.[2]

Canada helped Washington consolidate a coup that sparked a furious popular backlash. Ottawa defended an unelected Peruvian regime that suspended civil liberties and imposed a curfew while deploying troops to the streets. Security forces killed over sixty mostly Indigenous protesters.

At a special meeting of the Organization of American States hours after Castillo was arrested Canada's representative to the OAS noted, "Canada would like to express its deep concern over President Castillo's attempt to dissolve congress and establish a government of exception in Peru. Such destabilizing actions run directly counter to the recommendation of the OAS high level group and risk jeopardizing Peru's adherence to democratic norms."[3] According to the Canadian government, the ouster of the elected president was a step forward for democracy.

Castillo's ouster was justified on the grounds the former union leader declared an "exceptional emergency government" and sought to dissolve Congress to pre-empt its bid to impeach him. The constitutional legitimacy of Castillo's actions was dubious. But his opponents' plan also undercut constitutional norms and they wanted the vice president to rule for the remaining of Castillo's four-and-a-half-year term. He at least called for immediate elections. Additionally, Castillo's approval rating was significantly higher than the Congress that removed him (30% versus 10%).[4]

Global Affairs and Canada's ambassador to Peru, Louis Marcotte, worked hard to shore up support for Dina Boluarte's replacement 'usurper' government. In the two months after Castillo's ouster Marcotte met president Boluarte, the foreign minister, vulnerable populations minister, production minister, and mining minister. It is rare for a Canadian ambassador to have so much contact with top officials of any government. The diplomatic activity reflected Ottawa's commitment to consolidating the shaky coup government, which was rejected by many regional governments and had multiple ministers resign.

The diplomatic encounters were also an indirect endorsement of Boluarte's repression. Security forces shot hundreds and detained many more. Sixty were killed.

Amidst large protests a week after Castillo's ouster, Marcotte met new foreign minister Ana Cecilia Gervasi, tweeting a photo with the message: "Today with Minister Gervasi, reiterated support for the transition government of President Boluarte to create consensus leading to transparent and fair elections that will bring social peace. Condemned violence and affirmed the right to peaceful assembly."[5] Simultaneously, Gervasi released a statement to the media, reported CBC, about meeting Marcotte, which "reiterated Peru's gratitude for the commitment of his country to work with President Dina Boluarte."[6] Three days later global affairs minister Mélanie Joly bolstered Canada's support for Boluarte tweeting, "Spoke with Peru's Foreign Minister, Ana Cecilia Gervasi, to reiterate our support for the transitional government of President Boluarte." Joly and Marcotte's moves followed similar moves by the US. Secretary of state Antony Blinken called Boluarte and US ambassador Lisa Kenna met her about the same time.[7] On December 23, ambassador Marcotte

tweeted, "I met today with President Boluarte to reiterate Canada's commitment to continue strengthening
the relation and to support Human Rights and transparent and fair elections."

Most of the Hemisphere took a different tack. In
"Canada takes sides as hemisphere splits over who
rules Peru," the CBC's Evan Dyer reported nine days
after Castillo was ousted that the US, Brazil, Ecuador,
Panama, Chile, Uruguay and Costa Rica expressed
support for Boluarte while Mexico, Argentina, Bolivia,
Dominica, Grenada, Saint Lucia, Saint Vincent and the
Grenadines, Saint Kitts and Nevis, Antigua, Barbuda,
Cuba, Nicaragua, Honduras, Venezuela, and Colombia
all expressed some opposition to Castillo's ouster.[8]

While Canada blamed Castillo for the political
crisis, other governments in the region criticized the
Peruvian opposition for not allowing Castillo to gov-
ern. His opponent in the second round of the presidential election, Keiko Fujimori, refused to even recognize
Castillo's election victory while the media and business elite attacked Castillo viciously. The big business
National Society of Industries vowed to "throw out
communism" by making the country ungovernable
and congress repeatedly sought to impeach Castillo.
For its part, the military demanded (successfully) the
removal of leftist cabinet members.[9]

The military and police brutally suppressed the
uprising against the elected president's removal.
Ottawa assisted the elitist and racist reactionary forces.

Conquest

Perú

you can
find relief
in lima

but not in
puno or
ayacucho

the poor
decry
castillo's

fate and
claim
we stole

the light
of all
creation

A Poem by Rob Rolfe

VENEZUELA, 2017 TO THE PRESENT

Since 2017, the Trudeau government has engaged in a brazen effort to overthrow Venezuela's government. In a bid to elicit "regime change," Ottawa worked to isolate Caracas, imposed illegal sanctions, took the Maduro government to the International Criminal Court, financed an often-unsavoury opposition and decided that a marginal right-wing opposition politician was the country's legitimate president.

Prior to the election of Hugo Chávez in 1999 and the advent of the socialist-oriented Bolivarian Revolution, Venezuela was governed by an unaccountable US-backed oil oligarchy that ignored the demands of the poor majority and repressed them when they attempted to rise up and claim their rights, as evidenced by the 1989 *Caracazo* massacre.

Chávez's promise to redistribute Venezuela's oil wealth while standing up for his country's national interests vis-à-vis the US made him a hero to the poor majority and enemy of Washington. Under Chávez, Venezuela helped launch regional organizations such as the Bolivarian Alliance for the Peoples of Our America (ALBA) and Union of South American Nations (UNASUR) and offered affordable energy to countries in the Caribbean through the Petrocaribe program.

Chávez also forced multinational oil companies, which often paid little in royalties, to become minority partners with the state oil company PDVSA. This led ExxonMobil and Petro-Canada to abandon the country in 2007. Furthermore, Chávez's push to increase the state's role in gold extraction led to legal battles with Canadian mining companies such as Crystallex, Vannessa Ventures, Gold Reserve Inc., and Rusoro Mining. In 2007, Peter Munk, the founder of Barrick Gold and one of Canada's premier capitalists, wrote a letter to the *Financial Times* in which he called Chávez a "dangerous dictator" and compared his actions to Pol Pot, Slobodan Milosevic, Robert Mugabe, and Adolf Hitler.

In addition to forging a new, boldly assertive foreign policy, the Bolivarian Revolution empowered Venezuela's poor and working class for nearly two decades. During its first fifteen years, substantial gains were made in public health, reducing illiteracy and lessening inequality.[1] Even amidst a severe economic downturn, Nicolás Maduro's government built three million units of social housing.[2]

The Chávez-led government/movement also massively increased democratic space through community councils, new political parties, grassroots media, and worker cooperatives. Between 1998 and 2018, the Bolivarian Revolution won nineteen elections.[3] After almost every defeat, large swaths of the opposition cried foul and sought to oust the president through unconstitutional means. US and Canadian officials largely sided with the opposition.

Taking advantage of Chávez's death in 2013 and a huge drop in the price of oil, the Barack Obama administration instigated sanctions on Venezuela. Washington labeled the South American country a threat to US "national security."[4] Donald Trump ramped up sanctions and repeatedly threatened to invade.[5] Concurrently, the opposition attempted to assassinate Nicolás Maduro.[6]

A May 2018 presidential election demonstrated that Maduro and his PSUV party maintained considerable support. Even with the opposition boycott, the turnout was 40% and Maduro received a higher proportion of the overall vote than leaders in the US, Canada, and elsewhere. For instance, in 2019, Trudeau's Liberals received 33% of the vote with 66% of eligible voters casting their ballots, which amounted to 22% of the adult population. Maduro received 67% of votes cast with 41% of eligible voters participating, which equaled 27% of the population.

Despite the complicated political situation, Canadian officials leveled over-the-top criticism against Venezuela's government. Trudeau repeatedly called Maduro a "brutal dictator" while foreign minister Chrystia Freeland said he was "robbing the Venezuelan people of their fundamental democratic rights."[7] Ottawa supported efforts to condemn Venezuela at the Organization of American States (OAS) and in 2018 requested the International Criminal Court (ICC) investigate the Maduro government. Supported by five like-minded South American nations, it was the first time a member state was brought before the ICC's chief prosecutor by other members.[8] But, Ottawa stayed mum about far worse human rights violations in Mexico, Honduras, and Colombia.[9]

Canada founded the anti-Maduro Lima Group coalition with Peru. Amidst discussions between the two countries' foreign ministers in spring 2017, Trudeau called his Peruvian counterpart, Pedro Pablo Kuczynski, to "stress the need for dialogue and respect for the democratic rights of Venezuelan citizens, as enshrined in the charter of the Organization of American States and the Inter-American Democratic Charter."[10] But the Lima Group was established in August 2017 as a structure outside of the OAS largely because that organization's members refused to back Washington and Ottawa's bid to interfere in Venezuelan affairs, which they believed defied the OAS' charter.

Canada was maybe the most active member of the coalition of governments opposed to Venezuela's elected government. Freeland participated in a half dozen meetings of the Lima Group and she repeatedly prodded Caribbean and Central American countries to join the Lima Group's anti-Maduro efforts.[11] The second Lima Group meeting, held in Toronto in October 2017, urged regional governments to take steps to "further isolate" Venezuela.[12]

Canadian officials even backed talk of an invasion which other members opposed. Eleven of the fourteen members of the Lima Group backed a September 2018 statement distancing the alliance from "any type of action or declaration that implies military intervention" after

OAS chief Luis Almagro stated: "As for military inter-vention to overthrow the Nicolas Maduro regime, I think we should not rule out any option … diplomacy remains the first option but we can't exclude any action."[13] Canada, Guyana, and Colombia refused to criticize the head of the OAS' musings about an invasion of Venezuela.

Canadian diplomats played an important role in uniting large swaths of the Venezuelan opposition behind a US-backed plan to ratchet up tensions by proclaiming the new head of the opposition-dom-inated National Assembly, Juan Guaidó, president. The Canadian Press quoted a Canadian diplomat saying they helped Guaidó "facilitate conversations with people that were out of the country and inside the country," while the *Globe and Mail* reported that "Freeland spoke with Juan Guaidó to congratulate him on unifying opposition forces in Venezuela, two weeks before he declared himself interim presi-dent" in January 2019.[14] Canadian diplomats spent "months," reported the Canadian Press, coordinating the plan with the hard-line opposition. In a story titled "Anti-Maduro coalition grew from secret talks," the Associated Press reported on Canada's "key role" in building international diplomatic support for claiming a relatively marginal National Assembly member was Venezuela's president.[15] Alongside Washington and a number of right-leaning Latin American governments, Ottawa immediately recognized Guaidó after he pro-claimed himself president at a rally. At the opening of the Lima Group meeting in Ottawa after Guaidó's presidential declaration, Trudeau declared, "the international community must immediately unite behind the interim president."

The PM called the leaders of France, Spain, Paraguay, Ireland, and Italy, as well as the International Monetary Fund and the European Union, to convince them to join Canada's campaign against Venezuela.[16] In a May 2019 conversation with Spanish prime minister Pedro Sánchez, Venezuela was the only subject mentioned in the official press release about the call.[17] Venezuela was also on the agenda during Japanese prime minister Shinzo Abe's visit to Ottawa in April 2019. The post-meeting release noted, "during the visit, Prime Minister Abe announced Japan's endorsement of the Ottawa Declaration on Venezuela."[18] Produced at a February 2019 meeting of the Lima Group, the "Ottawa Declaration" called on Venezuela's armed forces "to demonstrate their loyalty to the interim president" and remove the elected president.[19]

On April 30, Guaidó, opposition politician Leopoldo López (who was given a thirteen-year jail sentence for inciting and planning violence during the 2014 "guarimbas" protests), and others sought to stoke a military uprising in Caracas. Hours into the early morning effort, Freeland tweeted, "watching events today in Venezuela very closely. The safety and security of Juan Guaidó and Leopoldo López must be guaranteed. Venezuelans who peacefully support Interim President Guaidó must do so without fear of intimidation or violence."[20] She followed that up with a statement to the press noting, "Venezuelans are in the streets today demonstrating their desire for a return to democracy even in the face of a violent crackdown. Canada commends their courage and we call on the Maduro regime to step aside now."[21] Then Freeland put out a video calling on Venezuelans to rise up and requested an emergency video conference meeting of the Lima Group.[22] Later that evening, the coalition issued a statement labelling the attempted putsch an effort "to restore democracy" and demanded the military "cease being instruments of the illegitimate regime for the oppression of the Venezuelan people."[23]

Guaidó was officially dethroned as leader of Venezuela's National Assembly (the matter was contested) in January 2020. Two weeks later, Guaidó sought to reaffirm his international backing. He was fêted in Ottawa, meeting the prime minister, international development minister and foreign minister. Trudeau declared, "I commend Interim President Guaidó for the courage and leadership he has shown in his efforts to return democracy to Venezuela, and I offer Canada's continued support."[24]

Over a two-year period, Ottawa severed diplomatic relations with Caracas. Following Washington's lead, Ottawa imposed four rounds of sanctions on Venezuelan officials.[25] In September 2017, the elected president, vice president, head of the electoral board, and thirty seven other officials had their assets in Canada frozen and Canadians were barred from having financial relations with these individuals. When forty-three individuals were added to a list of seventy leaders, Canada had already sanctioned CBC reported in April 2019 that the sanctions aimed to "punish Venezuelan judges who rubber-stamped Maduro's moves" and "lower-ranking police officials who took prominent roles in suppressing the attempt by Venezuela's opposition to bring humanitarian aid into the country on February 23."[26]

The real objective of the sanctions was to help squeeze the economy to precipitate regime change. While ostensibly targeted at individuals, Canadian sanctions deterred companies from doing business in Venezuela. They also helped legitimate more devastating US actions.

The Venezuelan government responded to Canadian sanctions by denouncing Ottawa's "alliance with war criminals that have declared their intention to destroy the Venezuelan economy to inflict suffering on the people and loot the country's riches."[27] A Center for Economic and Policy Research report gave credence to this perspective. Written by Jeffrey Sachs and Mark Weisbrot, "Economic Sanctions as Collective Punishment: The Case of Venezuela" concluded that 40,000 Venezuelans may have died in 2017 and 2018 as a result of US sanctions.[28] A July 2019 *Financial Times* story titled "Venezuela sanctions fuel famine fears" and a *New York Times* op-ed that month titled "Misguided sanctions hurt Venezuelans" highlighted their growing impact.

Unilateral sanctions violate the UN charter. Additionally, the UN Human Rights Council passed a resolution condemning the economic sanctions the US and Canada adopted against Venezuela.[29] It urged "states to refrain from imposing unilateral coercive measures (and) condemns the continued unilateral application and enforcement by certain powers of such measures as tools of political or economic pressure."[30] For its part, Caracas called Canada's move a "blatant violation of the most fundamental rules of International Law."[31]

Canadian diplomats were encouraged to play up human rights violations in Venezuela. A 27-page Global Affairs report uncovered by the *Globe and Mail* noted, "Canada should maintain the embassy's prominent position as a champion of human-rights defenders." Alluding to the hostility engendered by its interference in that country's affairs, the partially redacted 2017 report recommended that Canadian officials also "develop and implement strategies to minimize the impact of attacks by the government in response to Canada's human rights statements and activities."[32]

Ottawa worked to amplify oppositional voices inside Venezuela. In 2017, outgoing Canadian ambassador Ben Rowswell told the *Ottawa Citizen*: "We established quite a significant internet presence inside Venezuela, so that we could then engage tens of thousands of Venezuelan citizens in a conversation on human rights. We became one of the most vocal embassies in speaking out on human rights issues and encouraging Venezuelans to speak out."[33]

During Rowswell's tenure at the embassy, Canada financed NGOs with the expressed objective of embarrassing the government internationally. According to the government's response to a July 2017 Standing Senate Committee on Foreign Affairs and International Trade report on Venezuela, "CFLI [Canada Fund for Local Initiatives] programming includes support for a local NGO documenting the risks to journalists and freedom of expression in Venezuela, in order to provide important statistical evidence to the national and international community on the worsening condition of basic freedoms in the country."[34] Another CFLI initiative funded during Rowswell's tenure in Caracas "enabled Venezuelan citizens to anonymously register and denounce corruption abuses by government officials and police through a mobile phone application."[35]

In line with its policy of amplifying oppositional voices, the Canadian Embassy in Caracas co-sponsored an annual Human Rights Award with the Centro para la Paz y los Derechos Humanos, whose director, Raúl Herrera, repeatedly denounced the Venezuelan government. In late 2017 Herrera said, "the Venezuelan State systematically and repeatedly violates the Human Rights of Venezuelans and political prisoners."[36]

The "Human Rights Prize" was designed to amplify and bestow legitimacy on anti-government voices. The winner received a "tour of several cities in Venezuela to share his or her experiences with other organizations promoting human rights" and a trip to Canada to meet with "human rights authorities and organizations."[37] They generally presented to Canadian Parliamentary Committees and garnered media attention. The Venezuelan NGOs most quoted in the Canadian media criticizing the country's human rights situation—Provea, Foro Penal, CODEVIDA, Observatorio Venezolano de la Conflictividad, Observatorio Venezolano de Prisiones, etc.—had been formally recognized by the Canadian Embassy.

In March 2018, the embassy gave its Human Rights Award to Francisco Valencia, director of the Coalición de Organizaciones por el Derecho a la Salud y la Vida (CODEVIDA). Numerous media outlets reported on the award given to an aggressive opponent of the Venezuelan government.[38] "I believe that we are facing a criminal State," Valencia told Crisis en Venezuela.[39] In July 2018 Valencia spoke in Ottawa and was profiled by the *Globe and Mail*. "Canada actually is, in my view, the country that denounced the most the violation of human rights in Venezuela … and was the most helpful with financing towards humanitarian issues," explained Valencia, who also told that paper he was "the target of threats from the government."[40]

In another example of an anti-government figure invited to Ottawa, the former mayor of metropolitan Caracas, Antonio Ledezma, called for "humanitarian intervention" before the Subcommittee on International Human Rights of the Standing Committee on Foreign Affairs and International Development.[41] In September 2018 Ledezma said, "if the international community does not urgently activate the principle of humanitarian intervention for Venezuela—which developed the concept of the responsibility to protect—they will have to settle for sending Venezuelans a resolution of condolence with which we will not revive the thousands of human beings who will lose their lives in the middle of this genocide sponsored by Maduro."[42] In November of the previous year, Ledezma escaped house arrest and fled the country.[43]

Ottawa allied with some of the most anti-democratic, hardline, and electorally marginal elements of Venezuela's opposition. Guaidó's Voluntad Popular (VP) party repeatedly instigated violent protests. Not long after the Democratic Unity Roundtable opposition coalition presidential candidate Henrique Capriles effectively conceded defeat in January 2014, VP leader Leopoldo López launched La Salida (exit/departure) in a bid to oust Maduro. VP activists formed the shock troops of "guarimbas" protests that left 43 Venezuelans dead, 800 hurt and a great deal of property damaged in 2014.[44] Dozens more were killed in a new wave of VP-backed protests in 2017.

Effective at stoking violence, VP failed to win many votes. It took eight percent of the seats in the 2015 elections that saw the opposition win control of the National Assembly.[45] With 14 out of 167 deputies in the Assembly, it won the fourth most seats in the Democratic Unity Roundtable coalition.[46] In the December 2012 regional elections VP was the sixth most successful party and did little better in the next year's municipal elections.

VP was founded at the end of 2009 by López, a politician who "has long had close contact with American diplomats" according to *The Wall Street*

Journal.[47] A great-great-grand nephew of independence leader Simón Bolívar, grandson of a former cabinet member and great-grandson of a president, López was schooled at Harvard's Kennedy School of Government.[48] Between 2000 and 2008, López was the relatively successful and popular mayor of the affluent 65,000 person Caracas municipality of Chacao.

During the 2002 military coup, López "orchestrated the public protests against Chávez and…played a central role in the citizen's arrest of Chávez's interior minister."[49] As stated earlier, he was convicted of inciting violence during the 2014 "guarimbas" and sentenced to thirteen years in jail.[50]

Canadian officials had significant contact with López's emissaries and party. The Canadian Embassy in Caracas worked with VP officials pushing for the overthrow of the elected government. The leader of VP in Yaracuy state, Gabriel Gallo, was runner-up for the embassy's 2015 human rights award.[51] A coordinator of the Foro Penal NGO, Gallo was also photographed with ambassador Ben Rowswell at the embassy's 2017 human rights prize ceremony.[52]

A slew of VP representatives visited Ottawa during this period. In May 2017, Trudeau met Lilian Tintori, wife of VP leader López. Tintori acted as an emissary for López, who couldn't travel to Ottawa because he was convicted of inciting violence during the "guarimbas" protests in 2014.

Three months earlier, Tintori met US president Donald Trump and *The Guardian* reported on her role in building international support for the plan to anoint VP deputy Guaidó interim president.[53]

In response, Venezuela's foreign affairs minister Delcy Rodríguez described Tintori as an "agent of intervention" who claims the "false position of victim" while she's aligned with "fascist" forces in Venezuela.[54] According to a series of reports, López was the key Venezuelan organizer of the plan to anoint Guaidó interim president.[55]

Canada strengthened VP's hardline position within the opposition. A February 2019 *Wall Street Journal* article titled "'What the Hell Is Going On?' How a Small Group Seized Control of Venezuela's Opposition" noted that leading opposition figures on stage with Guaidó when he declared himself interim president had no idea of his plan despite it being reliant on the Democratic Unity Roundtable's agreement to rotate the National Assembly presidency within the coalition.[56] (VP's turn came due in January 2019.)

Canada's "special coordinator for Venezuela" worked with VP and the opposition. From fall 2017 through 2020, Allan Culham was Canada's Special Advisor on Venezuela. Canadian taxpayers paid hundreds of thousands of dollars to the hardline pro-corporate, pro-Washington, former diplomat to coordinate the government's bid to oust Venezuela's government.

A former Canadian ambassador to Venezuela, El Salvador, Guatemala, and the Organization of American States, Culham described his affinity for López after retiring from the civil service in 2015.

Canada's Special Advisor on Venezuela wrote, "I met [Leopoldo] when he was the mayor of the Caracas municipality of Chacao where the Canadian Embassy is located. He too became a good friend and a useful contact in trying to understand the many political realities of Venezuela."[57]

During his time as ambassador to Venezuela from 2002 to 2005, Culham was hostile to Hugo Chávez's government. According to a WikiLeaks publication of US diplomatic messages, "Canadian Ambassador Culham expressed surprise at the tone of Chavez's statements during his weekly television and radio show 'Hello President' on February 15 [2004]. Culham observed that Chavez's rhetoric was as tough as he had ever heard him. 'He sounded like a bully,' said Culham, more intransigent and more aggressive."[58]

The US cable quoted Culham criticizing the national electoral council and speaking positively about the group overseeing a presidential recall referendum targeting Chávez. "Culham added that Sumate is impressive, transparent, and run entirely by volunteers," it noted. The name of then head of Súmate, Maria Corina Machado, was on a list of people who endorsed the April 2002 military coup against Chavez, for which she faced charges of treason.[59]

Ottawa passively supported the military detaining Chávez and imposing an unelected government. The 2002 coup lasted only two days before popular demonstrations, a split within the army, and international condemnation returned Chávez. While most Latin

American leaders condemned the coup, Canadian diplomats were silent. "In the Venezuelan coup in 2002, Canada maintained a low profile, probably because it was sensitive to the United States ambivalence towards Venezuelan president Hugo Chavez," writes Flavie Major in *Promoting Democracy in the Americas.*

Culham presumably coordinated his bid to oust Maduro with the Venezuela Task Force at Global Affairs. In a further sign of the brazenness of their campaign to oust Maduro's government, the Professional Association of Foreign Service Officers gave Patricia Atkinson, Head of the Venezuela Task Force at Global Affairs, its Foreign Service Officers award in June 2019.[60] The write-up explained, "Patricia, and the superb team she assembled and led, supported the Minister's engagement and played key roles in the substance and organization of 11 meetings of the 13 country Lima group which coordinates action on Venezuela. She assisted in developing three rounds of sanctions against the regime."[61]

When it comes to Venezuela, successive Canadian governments have aligned themselves against democratic processes of change and supported hardline right-wing opposition elements in their efforts to destroy the Bolivarian Revolution. In *Canada in the World*, Tyler Shipley summed up the nature of Canada's role in post-1999 Venezuela succinctly: "Canada [has] actively participated in efforts to subvert and dismantle a process built by and for a large majority of Venezuelans."[62]

CONCLUSION

Why has there never been a coup in Canada? There's no Canadian Embassy in Ottawa.

Canadian leaders are keen to project the myth that Canada is a uniquely democratic actor on the world stage, with an exceptional history of supporting human rights and struggles for equality. This book has revealed that Ottawa's foreign policy is not driven by democracy, but by the interests of corporate Canada, which are often anathema to democracy.

By examining the history of Canadian support for military coups, this book explodes the myth that Canada promotes democracy around the world. In fact, Ottawa has repeatedly undermined elected, often progressive, governments and in doing so has helped destroy projects to build more equitable and democratic forms of governance across the globe.

By our calculation, the Canadian government has passively or actively backed over twenty coups. Ottawa has helped overthrow elected governments even when the social costs were, as anyone could have expected, enormous. To cite only a few examples: Mobutu's dictatorship lasted over three decades in Congo; thousands were killed after the 2004 coup in Haiti; and the 2014 ouster of Victor Yanukovych in Ukraine led to a civil war and contributed to Russia's invasion in 2022. By backing the overthrow of Lumumba and Mobutu's rise to power, by participating in the coup against Aristide and propping up his successor, and by assisting in the removal of Yanukovych, the Canadian government helped set the stage for the horrors that followed.

Mirroring its support for coups abroad, Canada has a long history of undermining other nations' politics. British and French colonizers destroyed Indigenous governance structures, which often served First Nations well for hundreds of years. They liquidated Mi'kmaq leaders in the Maritimes and bombed First Nations chiefs into submission on the west coast.

Since Confederation, the federal government has undermined Indigenous governments in innumerable ways. In 1870 and 1885, for example, British and Canadian troops violently repressed two rebellions against the expansion of colonial rule into Western Canada. Louis Riel, a prominent leader of these resistance movements and the founder of Manitoba, was hanged by the Canadian government in 1885.

For a century Indian Agents oversaw politics on reserves and the *1876 Indian Act subverted Indigenous governance. To instill* dependence on *Indian Affairs,* the federal government-*imposed* band councils on hundreds of First Nations. The *Indian Act* undercut *direct democracy and* governing structures linked to distinct land and cultural practices. For over half a century women and hereditary chiefs were largely excluded from band council politics.

Despite regular paeans to "reconciliation," Ottawa continues to subvert First Nations self-governance and intervened to prevent more democratic decision-making. In recent years Canada has repeatedly jailed band council leaders. In 2008, for instance, the chief, deputy chief and four other members of the Kitchenuhmaykoosib Inninuwug (Big Trout Lake) council were imprisoned for their opposition to mining operations on their reserve 600 km north of Thunder Bay, Ontario.

A more subtle way to usurp Indigenous governance has been to impose third party management. It grants the federal government control of a reserve's finances.[1]

The Algonquins of Barriere Lake were placed under third party management and then the federal government sidelined the nation's leadership.[2] After years of struggle, Barriere Lake won a landmark revenue sharing and resource co-management agreement with the Federal and Provincial governments. Unhappy with the 1991 "Trilateral Agreement," Indian Affairs fomented division within a community that hunts, traps and harvests on 10,000 square kilometers north of Ottawa. Ottawa failed to pay Barriere Lake resource management fees under the "Trilateral Agreement" and imposed third party management on the reserve. They refused to recognize the Algonquin's Customary Chief and subsequently organized an election that a dozen in the community of 500 participated in.[3] For a time, the Canadian government-recognized Chief operated from a location far outside the community.

There is a wealth of scholarship on the ways in which Ottawa has dismantled Indigenous governance, but research into Canada's support for ousting governments around the world is lacking. This book aims to remedy that gap.

In addition to shining a light on Canadian foreign policy, this book aims to help readers better understand the coup process itself. Rarely do coups begin the day the leader or government is overthrown, and there are generally many opportunities to stop them. Successful coups, however, usually include economic, diplomatic, propaganda, and military dimensions.

To generate popular frustration with the targeted government, outside powers usually seek to "make the economy scream," as US president Richard Nixon declared when seeking to destabilize Salvador Allende's Chile.[4] This usually includes cutting off aid or bilateral and multilateral loans, and sometimes it means imposing sanctions. During the coup attempt against Venezuela, which Ottawa actively assisted, then US National Security Advisor John Bolton compared similar measures against the Maduro government to Darth Vader choking his victims in *Star Wars*.[5]

Invariably, coup attempts also include a disinformation campaign. In Canada, the tactic of using disinformation against enemies of state goes back many years. During the 1885 Northwest rebellion on the prairies, for example, Ottawa took over local newspapers and used them to spread racist propaganda and hinder local support for the resistors.[6] When it comes to international coup attempts, disinformation campaigns serve a similar purpose. The human rights violations of the targeted government are exaggerated while the nation's leader is demonized as corrupt, authoritarian, and evil. There is also usually some effort to promote or organize opposition protests. The US and Canada often fund civil society groups and coordinate with opposition politicians. Sometimes, as was the case in Venezuela, they even help create a parallel leadership.

Generally, there is an effort to isolate the government diplomatically. The targeted government is criticized in international forums and may be blocked from participating in international gatherings. Sometimes a multistate alliance is created to criticize the targeted state and isolate them further on the world stage. At the same time, destabilization campaigns are devised in order to stoke unrest and legitimate military intervention. Sometimes foreign troops intervene but it is usually the targeted country's armed forces, which is why the US and Canadian militaries seek influence with their counterparts in other countries by training them.

Much like how First Nations were targeted by the state to acquire their land and wealth, governments targeted for coups have often pursued political, economic, and social reforms that anger the corporate set. In many cases, Canadian-backed coups have led to the reversal of these reforms and created direct money-making opportunities. After Pinochet's 1973 coup against Allende, Timothy David Clark notes, "Canadian mining companies were leaders in the stampede of foreign investment to Chile.

Between 1974 and 2003, Canada was the third-largest single investor in the country, behind the United States and Spain, with Spain surpassing Canada only towards the end of the 1990s."[7] In the three decades after Allende was overthrown, Canadian companies owned most of Chile's largest mining projects.

It must also be said that narrow corporate interests rarely drive a coup. Broader economic, racial and geostrategic dimensions usually shape policy toward targeted nations as well. For example, ousting Congo's Patrice Lumumba, Uganda's Milton Obote and Ghana's Kwame Nkrumah was partly about stunting these leaders' efforts to dismantle colonial structures and foster pan-African unity. One can identify a similar dynamic at play in recent coups in Latin America. Undercutting regional integration was a factor in the coups in Bolivia, Honduras, and Brazil as well as the failed bid to oust the Venezuelan government.

Some coups are largely about geopolitics. Ottawa wanted to be rid of Viktor Yanukovych because he promoted cordial relations with Moscow and opposed Ukraine joining NATO. In this case, an organized ethnic lobby was also an influential force in promoting Canada's bid to subvert the elected Yanukovych. The Ukrainian Canadian Congress, which represents Western Ukrainian nationalists, pushed Ottawa to act against Yanukovych. A similar force contributed to Canada's effort to sabotage Palestinian elections as the Israel lobby in Canada is well-financed and organized around a specific political ideology.

The coup in Haiti was shaped by a particularly virulent form of racism. Since its 1804 Revolution, white supremacist forces have sought to humiliate the country's impoverished Black masses and Canada threw its weight behind their goals by helping overthrow a learned, polyglot Black president hated by the country's light-skinned elite.

In all the coups documented in this book, Ottawa worked in tandem with the US government. However, that does not mean Ottawa was coerced into supporting these anti-democratic forces. The Canadian elite does not require pressure from Washington to dispossess and disempower Indigenous nations. Canadian leaders generally participated in the coups happily, which speaks to how elite Canadian interests are served by the US empire. In short, Canada's ruling class views the world much like their US counterparts do and profits from global exploitation in a similar way.

If we are serious about democracy, the correct prescription is to First Do No Harm. Rather than seeking to make Canada a force for promoting elections, we need to restrain Ottawa's ability to subvert democracy around the world. Fortunately, this approach is low cost. It does not require new financial contributions or interventions and is also in line with international law. Non-interference in other countries' affairs is an important principle of international law. Article 2 (7) of the UN Charter states that "nothing should authorize intervention in matters essentially within the domestic jurisdiction of any state."[8] Furthermore, the concept of self-determination is a core principle of the UN Charter and International Covenant on Civil and Political Rights.

In recent years, the Canadian government and media have devoted significant attention to China and Russia's purported interference in Canadian democracy. For instance, the Trudeau government established a special task force of CSIS, RCMP, CSE, and Global Affairs officials to monitor potential threats to Canada's electoral system.[9] While no foreign government should meddle in another country's political or electoral system, Ottawa has little standing to moralize on the subject. As outlined throughout this book, Canada has interfered in the political and electoral systems of many countries, backing certain leaders over others and helping shape those countries' politics to fit Ottawa's preferences. Simply put, if foreign meddling in a country's sovereign affairs is unconscionable to our leadership, then they should stop doing it elsewhere.

Hopefully this book assists readers in evaluating officials' claims on both the topics in question and other international issues. Indirectly, this book challenges the notion that Ottawa's conflict with other states is about democracy or authoritarianism. Are we really to believe Canadian officials are concerned about democracy in China, Russia, or Iran when they've repeatedly subverted elected governments?

This book is about Canada's role in overthrowing democracy, but more broadly, it is a handbook for democracy. Democracy requires an informed public, and Canadians cannot demand better of their government if they do not understand what that government is doing.

NOTES

Introduction

1. Quoted in Ernie Regehr, *Arms Canada: The Deadly Business of Military Exports* (Toronto: Lorimer, 1987), 39.

2. Quoted in Jeremy Kinsman, "Who is My Neighbour?: Trudeau and Foreign Policy," *International Journal*, vol. 57, no. 1, 2002, 73.

3. "Minister Baird Concludes Successful Visit to the Gulf Region News Release," *Government of Canada*, Nov. 22, 2011 (https://www.canada.ca/en/news/archive/2011/11/minister-baird-concludes-successful-visit-gulf-region.html).

4. "It's not about diaspora: Freeland explains why Canada supports Ukraine," *Ukrinform*, Feb. 11, 2019 (https://www.ukrinform.net/rubric-polytics/2810721-its-not-about-diaspora-freeland-explains-why-canada-supports-ukraine.html).

Iran, 1953

1. External Affairs file 50152 - 40 - 55 volume 5859

2. Stephen Kinzer, *All the Shah's Men: An American Coup and the Roots of Middle East Terror* (Hoboken: John Wiley & Sons, 2004), 80.

3. Ibid., 80.

4. Ibid., 87.

5. Hansard May 14 1951, 3002.

6. Hansard Oct 22 1951, 253.

7. Quoted in Artemy Kalinovsky, "The Soviet Union and Mossadeq: A Research Note," Iranian Studies, vol. 47, no. 3, 2014, pp. 402.

8. Netherton, In/Security, 345.

9. Kinzer, op. cit.., 160.

10. Ibid.

11. External Affairs file 50152 - 40 - 31, vol. 5859.

12. External Affairs file 50152 - 40 - 42, vol. 5859.

13. External Affairs file 50152 - 40 - 42, vol. 5859.

14. External Affairs file 50152 - 40 - 31, vol. 5859.

15. Foreign relations of Canada (http://en.wikipedia.org/wiki/Foreign_relations_of_Canada).

16. Tyler Shipley, *Canada in the World: Settler Capitalism and the Colonial Imagination* (Winnipeg: Fernwood Publishing, 2020), 307.

Colombia, 1953

1. Stefano Tijerina, "One Size Fits All? Canadian Development Assistance to Colombia, 1953-1972," in *A Samaritan State Revisited: Historical Perspectives on Canadian Foreign Aid* (Calgary: University of Calgary Press, 2019), 128.

2. Ibid., 129-130.

3. Tijerina, "Securing the Expansion of Capitalism in Colombia: Canadair and the Military Regime of General Gustavo Rojas Pinilla (1953–1957)," in *Big Business and Dictatorships in Latin America: A Transnational History of Profits and Repression* (London: Palgrave Macmillan, 2020), 350.

4. Tijerina, "One Size Fits All?," 130.

5. Tijerina, "Securing the Expansion of Capitalism," 366.

6. Ibid., 365.

7. Ibid., 366.

Guatemala, 1954

1. Quoted in W. George Lovell, "Memories of Fire: Eduardo Galeano and the Geography of Guatemala," *Geoforum* 37, no. 1, (2006), 35.

2. Stephen Schlesinger and Stephen Kinzer, *Bitter Fruit: The Story of the American Coup in Guatemala* (Cambridge: David Rockefeller Center for Latin American Studies, 2005), 75.

3. Ibid., 12.

4. Ibid., 73.

5. Noam Chomsky, *Year 501: The Conquest Continues* (Boston: South End Press, 1999), 37.

6. Quoted in Richard Sanders, "Exclusive Series on Canadian Ties to U.S. Empire: Lester Pearson and the Myth of Canada as Peaceable Kingdom (Part 1)," *CovertAction Magazine*, Mar. 30, 2021.

7. James Francis Rochlin, *Discovering the Americas: The Evolution of Canadian Foreign Policy Towards Latin America* (Vancouver: UBC Press, 1994), 35.

8. Peter McFarlane, *Northern Shadows: Canadians in Central America* (Toronto: Between the Lines, 1989), 98.

9. Ibid., 99.

10. Ibid., 99.

11. Ibid., 100.

12. 1954 Guatemalan coup d'état (http://en.wikipedia.org/wiki/ 1954_Guatemalan_coup_d%27%C3%A9tat).

The Democratic Republic of Congo, 1961

1. Robin S. Gendron, *Towards a Francophone Community: Canada's Relations with France and French Africa, 1945-1968*, 80.

2. Ama Biney, "War in Congo," *Frontier Weekly*, vol. 45, 2012.

3. H. Basil Robinson, *Diefenbaker's World: A Populist in Foreign Affairs* (Toronto: University of Toronto Press, 1989), 148.

4. Yves Engler, *Canada in Africa: 300 Years of Aid and Exploitation* (Winnipeg: Fernwood Publishing, 2015), 120.

5. Susan Williams, *Who Killed Hammarskjold?: The UN, the Cold War and White Supremacy in Africa* (Oxford: Oxford University Press, 2014), 33.

6. Ludo de Witte, Ann Wright, *The Assassination of Lumumba*, (Verso Books, 2003), 15.

7. Alastair MacDonald Taylor, David Cox, J. L. Granatstein, *Peacekeeping: International Challenge and Canadian Response* (Toronto: Canadian Institute of International Affairs, 1968), 158.

8. Daniel Galvin, "A role for Canada in an African crisis: perceptions of the Congo crisis and motivations for Canadian participation," University of Guelph Dissertation, 2004, 91.

9. Ibid.

10. Kevin Spooner, *Canada, the Congo Crisis, and UN Peacekeeping* (UBC Press, 2010) 75.

11. J.P.R. Beauregard, "UN operations in the Congo 1960 – 1964," *Canadian Defense Quarterly*, Aug. 1989.

12. J.L. Granatstein and David Bercuson, *War and Peacekeeping: From South Africa to the Gulf-Canada's Limited Wars* (Toronto: Key Porter Books, 1991), 219.

13. Fred Gaffen, *In the eye of the storm: A history of Canadian peacekeeping* (Univeristy of Toronto Press, 1987), 227; Sean Maloney, *Canada and UN Peacekeeping: Cold War by Other Means, 1945-1970* (Vanwell, 2002) 122.

14. Galvin, op. cit., 86.

15. Galvin, op. cit., 40.

16. Galvin, op. cit., 43.

17. Spooner, op. cit., 87-88.

18. Taylor et al, op. cit., 161.

19. Spooner, op. cit., 59.

20. Spooner, op. cit., 76.

21. Ibid.

22. Kevin Spooner, "Just West of Neutral: Canadian Objectivity and Peacekeeping during the Congo Crisis, 1960-61," *Canadian Journal of African Studies*, vol. 43, Issue 2, 2009.

23. Issaka K. Souare, *Africa in the United Nations System, 1945-2005* (London: Adonis & Abbey, 2006), 97.

24. Souare, *Africa in the United Nations System*, 97.

25. Frank Villafana, *Cold War in the Congo: The Confrontation of Cuban Military Forces*, 1960-1967 (Oxfordshire: Routledge, 2017), 25.

26. William Blum, *Killing Hope: US Military and CIA Interventions Since World War II* (Bloomsbury Academic, 2022), 158.

27. William J. Durch, *The Evolution of UN peacekeeping: case studies and comparative analysis* (Palgrave Macmillan, 1993) 321.

28. Lori Lyn Bogle, *Hot Wars of the Cold Wars* (*The Cold War*, vol. 3), (Routledge, 2001), 176.

29. Lise Namikas, *Battleground Africa: Cold War in the Congo, 1960–1965* (Stanford University Press, 2015), 89.

30. Ludo de Witte and Ann Wright, op. cit., 17.

31. Galvin, op. cit., 83.

32. Peter J. Schrader, *United States Foreign Policy Toward Africa: Incrementalism, Crisis and Change* (Cambridge: Cambridge University Press, 1994), 55.

33. Spooner, op. cit., 71; Namikas, op. cit., 88.

34. Spooner, op. cit., 89.

35. Ibid., 116.

36. Ibid.

37. Kevin A. Spooner, "The Diefenbaker Government and Foreign Policy in Africa" in *Reassessing the Rogue Tory: Canadian Foreign Relations in the Diefenbaker Era* (Vancouver: UBC Press, 2018), 202.

38. David C. *Reece, Special Trust and Confidence: Envoy Essay s in Canadian Diplomacy* (Carleton University Press, 1996), 111.

39. Gaffen, op. cit., 227.

40. Witte et al., op. cit., 149.

The Dominican Republic, 1963

1. Juan Bosch, *The Unfinished Experiment: Democracy in the Dominican Republic* (London: Pall Mall Press, 1966), ix.

2. Ibid., xi-xii.

3. Piero Gleijeses, *The Dominican Crisis: The 1965 Constitutionalist Revolt and American Intervention* (Baltimore: Johns Hopkins University Press, 1978), 258.

4. Gleijeses, *op. cit.*, 258.

5. Gleijeses, *op. cit.*, 258.

6. Gleijeses, *op. cit.*, 260.

7. Latin America Working Group, Letter, vol. 11, no. 8.

8. Hansard, May 3, 1965, 831.

9. John Dirks, "Friendly Noises but Distant Neighbours: Pearson, Latin America, and the Caribbean," in *Mike's World: Lester B. Pearson and Canadian External Affairs* (Vancouver: UBC Press, 2017), 197.

10. Hansard, May 21, 1965, 1560.

11. Hansard, May 11, 1965, 1152.

12. Hansard, May 4, 1965, 887.

13. Hansard, May 28, 1965, 1777.

14. Robert Carty, *Perpetuating Poverty* (Betwen the Lines, 1981), 64; Latin America Working Group, Letter, vol. 3, no. 4.

15. John Dirks, op. cit., 198.

16. Hansard Apr. 29, 1965, 721.

17. Latin America Working Group, Letter, vol. 11, no. 8.

18. Robert Wright and Lana Wylie, *Our Place in the Sun: Canada and Cuba in the Castro Era* (University of Toronto Press, 2009), 136.

19. John Deverell, *Falconbridge: Portrait of a Canadian Mining Multinational* (Toronto: Lorimer, 1975), 130.

20. Deverell, op. cit., 132.

21. Wright, op. cit., 135.

Brazil, 1964

1. Felipe Pereira Loureiro, "The Alliance for Progress and President João Goulart's Three Year Plan: the deterioration of U.S.-Brazilian Relations in Cold War Brazil (1962)," in *Cold War History*, vol. 17, no. 1, 2017, 69.

2. Ibid., 70.

3. Ibid., 73.

4. Peter Kornbluh, "Brazil Marks 40th Anniversary of Military Coup" (https://nsarchive2.gwu.edu/NSAEBB/NSAEBB118/index.htm).

5. Barbosa, *Brazil and Canada in the Americas* (Halifax: Gorsebrook Research Institute, 2007), 44.

6. Latin America Working Group, Letter, vol. iv, no. 2.

7. *Last Post,* Mar. 1973, vol. 3, no. 2.

8. Ibid.

9. Arruda, *The Multinational Corporations and Brazil,* (Brazilian Studies, Latin America Research Unit, 1975), 94.

10. Latin America Working Group, Letter, vol. iv, no. 2.

11. Ibid.

12. *Last Post*, Mar. 1973, vol. 3, no. 2.

13. Robert Chodos, *Let Us Prey* (Toronto: Lorimer, 1974), 17.

Indonesia, 1965

1. David Webster, *Fire and the Full Moon: Canada and Indonesia in a Decolonizing World* (Vancouver: UBC Press, 2009), 142.

2. Ibid., 191.

3. Ibid., 149.

4. Ibid., 150.

5. Ibid.

6. Ibid., 141.

7. Ibid., 137.

8. Indonesian mass killings of 1965–66 (http://en.wikipedia.org/wiki/Indonesian_killings_of_1965%E2%80%931966).

9. Webster, op. cit., 152.

10. Ibid., 153.

11. Ibid., 154.

12. Jamie Swift and the Development Education Centre, *The Big Nickel: Inco at Home and Abroad* (Kitchener: Between the Lines, 1977), 88.

13. Ibid., 88.

14. David R. Morrison, *Aid and Ebb Tide: A History of CIDA and Canadian Development Assistance* (Waterloo: Wilfrid Laurier University Press, 2014), 74.

15. Kim Richard Nossal, *Rain Dancing: Sanctions in Canadian and Australian Foreign Policy* (Toronto: University of Toronto Press, 1994), 39.

16. Webster, op. cit., 151.

17. Ibid., 155.

Ghana, 1966

1. John P. Schlegel, *The Deceptive Ash: Bilingualism and Canadian Policy in Africa: 1957-1971*, (Lanham: University Press of America, 1978), 64.

2. Hansard, Mar. 17, 1966, 2808.

3. Christopher R. Kilford, *The Other Cold War: Canada's Military Assistance to the Developing World 1945-1975*, (Canadian Defence Academy Press, 2010), 154.

4. Canadian Institute for International Affairs, vol. V, no. 3.

5. Thomas A. Howell, *Ghana and Nkrumah* (Four Winds Press, 1972), 129/143

6. Schlegel, op. cit., 64.

7. Kilford, op. cit., 155.

8. Howell, op. cit., 175.

9. Schlegel, op. cit., 63.

10. Gary Hunt, "Recollections of the Canadian Armed Forces Training Team in Ghana, 1961-1968," *Canadian Defence Quarterly 18*, spring 1989.

11. Kilford, op. cit., 155.

12. Ibid., 142.

13. Ibid., 143.

14. Ibid., 160.

15. Schlegel, op. cit., 63.

16. Kilford, op. cit., 149.

17. Ibid.

18. Ibid., 151.

19. David E. Apter, *Ghana in Transition* (New Jersey: Princeton University Press, 1972), 337.

20. Kwame Nkrumah, *Dark Days in Ghana* (New York: International Publishers, 1968), 139-140.

Greece, 1967

1. Effie G. H. Pedaliu, "'A Discordant Note': NATO and the Greek Junta, 1967-1974," *Diplomacy & Statecraft*, vol. 22, 2011, 101.

2. Alexandros Nafpliotis, "'A gift from God': Anglo-Greek relations during the dictatorship of the Greek colonels," *The Historical Review*, vol. 11, 2014 70-71.

3. Jonathan Marshall, "Coups Inside NATO: A Disturbing History," *Consortium News*, July 27, 2016.

4. Christopher Grafos, "Canada's Greek Moment: Transnational Politics, Activists, and Spies During the Long Sixties," PhD Diss., (York University, 2016), 26.

5. Pedaliu, op. cit., 102.

6. Asa McKercher, *Canada and the World Since 1867* (London: Bloomsbury, 2019), 140.

7. Grafos, op. cit., 77.

8. Ibid., 64-65

9. Katherine L. Pendakis, "Migration, morals, and memory: political genealogies of a transnational Greek left," *Citizenship Studies*, vol. 22, no. 4, 2018, 424.

10. Ibid., 425.

11. Grafos, op. cit., 176.

12. Ibid., 90.

13. Ibid., 90.

14. Ibid., 111-112.

15. Pedaliu, op. cit., 116.

Uganda, 1971

1. Irving Gershenberg, "Slouching Towards Socialism: Obote's Uganda," *African Studies Review*, vol. 15, no. 1, 1972, 79.

2. Ali A. Mazrui, "Nkrumah, Obote and Vietnam," *Transition*, vol. 43, 1973, 38.

3. Mazrui, op. cit., 39.

4. Mazrui, op. cit., 38.

5 Mark Curtis, *Unpeople: Britain's Secret Human Rights Abuses*, (London, Vintage, 2004)

6. Ibid.

7. Gershenberg, op. cit., 81.

8. Deverell, *Falconbridge: Portrait of a Canadian Mining Multinational* (Toronto: Lorimer, 1975), 177.

9. Gershenberg, op. cit., 79.

10. Leo Louis Jacques, *African Pearls and Poisons: Idi Amin's Uganda; Kenya; Zaire's Pygmies* (AuthorHouse, 2013), 6.

Chile, 1973

1. Patricio Guzmán, Salvador Allende (https://icarusfilms.com/if-sal).

2. Salvador Allende, "Speech to the United Nations (excerpts)," *Marxists.org*, Dec. 4, 1972 (https://www.marxists.org/archive/allende/1972/december/04.htm).

3. Robert Clarke and Richard Swift, *Ties that Bind: Canada and the Third World* (Between the Lines, 1982).

4. James Rochlin, *Discovering the Americas: The Evolution of Canadian Foreign Policy Towards Policy towards Latin America* (UBC Press, 1994), 83.

5. Ibid., 88.

6. Shipley, *Canada in the World*, 272.

7. Owen Schalk, "What Will Gabriel Boric Mean for Canadian Mining in Chile?" (https://alborada.net/canada-chile-oric-trudeau-mining-extraction-capitalism/).

8. Latin America Working Group, Letter, vol. 4, Issue 1, P.6.

9. "Canada's NGO Radicals Confront the September 11th Coup," Sep. 11, 2013 (https://www.mediacoop.ca/story/canadas-ngo-radicals-confront-september-11th-coup/18849).

10. Jan Raska, 1973: Canada's Response to the Chilean Refugees (https://pier21.ca/research/immigration-history/canadas-response-chilean-crisis).

11. Michael Molloy, "When The Refugees Came" (https://opencanada.org/when-the-refugees-came-snapshots-from-five-compassionate-moments-in-canadas-history/#1970s-exodus-from-chile).

Peru, 1992

1. Charles D. Kenney, *Fujimori's Coup and the Breakdown of Democracy in Latin America* (Notre Dame: University of Notre Dame Press, 2004), 203-204.

2. Alfredo Schulte-Bockholt, *Corruption as Power: Criminal Governance in Peru during the Fujimori Era (1990-2000)* (Bern: Peter Lang, 2013), 93.

3. Conaghan, *Fujimori's Peru: Deception in the Public Sphere* (Pittsburgh: University of Pittsburgh Press, 2005), 9.

4. Kenney, *Fujimori's Coup*, 241.

5. José de Echave, "Canadian Mining Companies Investments in Peru: The Tambogrande Case and the Need to Implement Reforms," *CooperAcción*, Apr. 2005 (https://miningwatch.ca/sites/default/files/4perucasestudy.pdf.

6. Daviken Studnicki-Gizbert, "Canadian mining in Latin America (1990 to present): a provisional history," *Canadian Journal of Latin American and Caribbean Studies* 41, no. 1 (2016), pp. 95-113.

7. "Fujimori defends record in Peru," *United Press International* (https://www.upi.com/amp/Archives/1998/10/27/Fujimori-defends-record-in-Peru/9017909464400/).

Russia, 1993

1. Andrew Felkay, *Yeltsin's Russia and the West* (Westport: Prager Publishers, 2002), 78.

2. Alexander Buzgalin and Andrei Kolganov, *Bloody Oct. in Moscow: Political Repression in the Name of Reform* (New York: Monthly Review Press, 1994), 27.

3. Boris Kagarlitsky, *Russia Under Yeltsin and Putin: Neo-liberal Autocracy* (London: Pluto Press, 2002), 85.

4. Reddaway and Glinski, *The Tragedy of Russia's Reforms*, 371.

5. Brian Mulroney, *Memoirs: 1939-1993* (Toronto: McClelland & Steward Ltd, 2007), 985.

6. Jeremy Kinsman, "A skate with democracy," CBC (https://www.cbc.ca/news2/background/berlinwall/memories/f-vp-kinsman.html).

7. Mulroney, op. cit., 984.

8. Kim Campbell, *Time and Chance: The Political Memoirs of Canada's First Woman Prime Minister* (Toronto: Doubleday Canada Limited, 1996), 333.

9. Yuri Adjubei, "Russia: A Largely Untapped Potential," in *Foreign Investment in Russia and Other Soviet Successor States* (London: MacMillan Press Ltd, 1996), 140.

10. Ibid., 154-155.

11. Ibid., 49.

12. Alexander Panetta, "Chretien, Mulroney share memories of larger-than-life Yeltsin," *The Globe and Mail*, Apr. 23, 2007.

13. Kagarlitsky, op. cit., 77.

Haiti, 2004

1. Peter Hallward, *New Left Review*, May/June 2004 (https://archive.globalpolicy.org/us-military-expansion-and-intervention/haiti-8-7/34486.html).

2. Jooneed Khan, "Les Haïtiens iront finalement aux urnes dimanche prochain," *La presse*, May 17, 2000.

3. Jooneed Khan, "Attentat au siège des élections en Haïti Le Québec refuse toujours d'y envoyer des observateurs," *La presse*, May 19, 2000.

4. Peter McKenna, "Helping Haiti is a long-haul project," *Montreal Gazette*, Sep. 22, 1999.

5. Jooneed Khan, "L'opposition nomme un 'président provisoire' en Haïti," *La presse*, Feb. 7, 2001,

6. Jooneed Khan, "Élections haïtiennes: le dossier se complique," *La presse*, June, 6 2000.

7. Mike Trickey, "Canadian embassy attacked: Grenade lobbed into ambassador's yard in Haiti; no one hurt," *Montreal Gazette*, July 29, 2000.

8. Jooneed Khan, "Jean-Bertrand Aristide est de retour à la tête d'Haïti," *La presse*, Nov. 30, 2000.

9. Standing Senate Committee on Foreign Affairs and Trade, Number 010 l 3rd Session, Apr. 1, 2004 https://www.ourcommons.ca/documentviewer/en/37-3/FAIT/meeting-10/evidence

10. Peter Hallward, *Damming the Flood: Haiti and the Politics of Containment* (London: Verso, 2008), 86.

11. Ricardo A. S. Seitenfus, "Un golpe a la democracia: la caída de Aristide Book Reconstruir Haití: entre la esperanza y el tridente imperial" (https://www.jstor.org/stable/j.ctvtxw1x0.10).

12. (https://www.oas.org/en/media_center/press_release.asp?scodigo=e-118/03).

13. Kevin Edmonds, "CIDA Continues its History of Controversy in Haiti," *NACLA*, Jan. 24, 2013 (https://nacla.org/blog/2013/1/24/cida-continues-its-history-controvery-haiti); Justin Podur, *Haiti's New Dictatorship: The Coup, the Earthquake and the UN Occupation* (London: Pluto Press, 2012), 36.

14. Anthony Fenton, "Left, Right, Left, Right: Running off With Haiti's Democracy", Feb. 15, 2006 (https://znetwork.org/znetarticle/left-right-left-right-running-off-with-haitis-democracy-by-anthony-fenton/).

15. "Canadian Cooperation With Haiti: Reflecting on a Decade of 'Difficult Partnership'," Canadian International Development Agency, Dec. 2004 (https://publications.gc.ca/collections/collection_2014/maecd-dfatd/CD4-73-2004-eng.pdf).

16. Ansel Herz and Kim Ives, "WikiLeaked Cables Reveal Obsessive, Far-Reaching U.S. Campaign to Get and Keep Aristide Out of Haiti," *Haiti Liberte*, July 27, 2011.

17. Michel Vastel, "Haïti mise en tutelle par l'ONU?," *L'actualité*, Mar. 15, 2003 (https://lactualite.com/monde/haiti-mise-en-tutelle-par-lonu/).

18. Peter Hallward, op. cit., 125-126.

19. Peter Hallward, op. cit., 125.

20. Lisa Macha Saye, "The Haitian state: something alien," *Journal of Third World Studies*, vol. 27, no. 2, Fall 2010 (https://www.jstor.org/stable/45194711).

21. Jooneed Khan, "La Caricom fait part à Paul Martin de la popularité d'Aristide en Haïti," *La presse*, Jan. 13, 2004.

22. Isabelle Rodrigue, "Denis Coderre représentera le Canada lors d'une rencontre avec Aristide," *La presse canadienne*, Feb. 19, 2004.

23. SECURITY COUNCIL AUTHORIZES DEPLOYMENT OF MULTINATIONAL FORCE TO HAITI FOR 3 MONTHS, UNANIMOUSLY ADOPTING RESOLUTION 1529, Feb. 29 2004, Press Release SC/8015 (https://www.un.org/press/en/2004/sc8015.doc.htm).

24. Joint Task Force 2: Canada's elite fighters, *CBC News*, Sep. 15, 2010 (https://www.cbc.ca/news/canada/joint-task-force-2-canadas-elite-fighters-1.873657).

25. "US marines to follow Canadians into Haiti," *Al Jazeera*, Feb. 29, 2004 (http://www.aljazeera.com/archive/2004/02/200841014219644764.html).

26. Richard Sanders, "A Very Canadian Coup, The top 10 ways that Canada aided the 2004 coup in Haiti and helped subject Haitians to a brutal reign of terror," Apr. 1, 2010 (https://policyalternatives.ca/publications/monitor/very-canadian-coup).

27. Haiti drops $22b claim against France, Apr. 20, 2004 (https://gulfnews.com/uae/haiti-drops-22b-claim-against-france-1.320036).

28. "The Ransom: The Root of Haiti's Misery: Reparations to Enslavers," *The New York Times*, May 20, 2022.

Palestine, 2006

1. Mehdi Hasan and Dina Sayedahmed, "Blowback: How Israel Went From Helping Create Hamas to Bombing It," *The Intercept*, Feb. 19, 2018.

2. "Canada suspends funding to Palestinian Authority," Mar. 29, 2006 (https://reliefweb.int/report/occupied-palestinian-territory/canada-suspends-funding-palestinian-authority).

3. Carolynne Wheeler, "Palestinians warn Canada of necessity for dialogue," *The Globe and Mail*, Mar. 30 2007.

4. Paul McGeough, *Kill Khalid: The Failed Mossad Assassination of Khalid Mishal and the Rise of Hamas* (The New Press, 2009).

5. Alan Freeman, "Ottawa restores aid to Palestinian Authority," *The Globe and Mail*, July 24, 2007.

6. "Canada commits $300M in aid for Palestinians," *CTV News*, Dec. 17, 2007.

7. Mark Perry, "Dayton's mission: A reader's guide," Jan. 25. 2011 (https://www.aljazeera.com/news/2011/1/25/daytons-mission-a-readers-guide).

8. "Prime Minister Justin Trudeau speaks with Palestinian Authority President Mahmoud Abbas," *Government of Canada*, June 29 2021, (https://pm.gc.ca/en/news/).

Honduras, 2009

1. "Month of violence turns Honduras into world's most dangerous country for journalists," Apr. 2, 2010 (https://www.refworld.org/docid/4bc2cd2d2c.html).

2. Yves Engler, "Canada alone in opposing the return of Zelaya in Honduras," July 7, 2009 (https://canadiandimension.com/articles/view/canada-alone-in-opposing-the-return-of-zelaya-in-honduras.-heres-why).

3. Ibid.

4. Ibid.

5. Ibid.

6. Yves Engler, "Canadian media silent on resistance to Honduras coup," Aug. 17, 2009 (https://rabble.ca/general/canadian-media-silent-resistance-honduras-coup/).

7. Ibid.

8. Ibid.

9. "Honduran Elections Marred by Police Violence, Censorship, International Non-Recognition, CEPR Co-Director Says," Nov. 30, 2009 (https://cepr.net/press-release/honduran-elections-marred-by-violence/).

10. "Canada Congratulates Honduran People on Elections," News Release, Dec. 1, 2009 (https://www.canada.ca/en/news/archive/2009/12/canada-congratulates-honduran-people-elections.html).

11. "Statement by Minister of State Kent on Inauguration of Honduran President," News Release, Jan. 28, 2010 (https://www.canada.ca/en/news/archive/2010/01/statement-minister-state-kent-inauguration-honduran-president.html).

Ukraine, 2014
1. Philip P. Pan, "International observers say Ukrainian election was free and fair," *OSCE PA*, Feb. 9, 2010 (https://www.oscepa.org/en/news-a-media/press-releases/press-2010/international-observers-say-ukrainian-election-was-free-and-fair).
2. Harrison Samphir, "Why is a monument commemorating a Nazi SS division still standing outside Toronto?," *Canadian Dimension*, July 26, 2020 (http://canadiandimension.com/articles/view/why-is-a-monument-commemorating-a-nazi-ss-division-still-standing-outside-of-toronto).
3. Shipley, *Canada in the World*, 456.
4. "Harper begins symbolic trip to Ukraine," *CTV News*, Oct. 24, 2010 (https://www.ctvnews.ca/harper-begins-symbolic-trip-to-ukraine-1.566518).
5. Ukrainian Canadian Congress, "Ukrainian Canadian Congress (UCC) Welcomes Visit by PM to Ukraine: UCC Encourages Harper Government to Engage Ukraine on Key Issues," *Newswire*, Oct. 19, 2010 (https://www.newswire.ca/news-releases/ukrainian-canadian-congress-ucc-welcomes-visit-by-pm-to-ukraine-uccencourages-harper-government-to-engage-ukraine-on-key-issues-545883762.html).
6. "Stephen Harper stresses freedom in Ukraine," *The Globe and Mail*, Oct. 25, 2010.
7. "PM warns Ukraine's relations with Canada could be damaged," *The Globe and Mail*, Oct. 14, 2011.
8. "Stephen Harper calls out Ukraine leader to hold fair elections," *Toronto Sun*, Oct. 19, 2012.
9. "Minister Kenney concludes successful visit to Ukraine," *Government of Canada*, Mar. 4, 2013 (https://www.canada.ca/en/news/archive/2013/03/minister-kenney-concludes-successful-visit-ukraine.html.
10. Seumas Milne, "It's not Russia that's pushed Ukraine to the brink of war," *The Guardian*, Apr. 30, 2014.
11. Ibid.
12. "Canadian interference in Ukrainian affairs reaches epic proportions," Feb. 9, 2022 (https://yvesengler.com/2022/02/09/canadian-interference-in-ukrainian-affairs-reaches-epic-proportions/).
13. "Maybe the story is more complex than Russia bad, Canada good," Jan. 24, 2022 (https://yvesengler.com/2022/01/24/maybe-the-story-is-more-complex-than-russia-bad-canada-good/).

14. President Barack Obama spent "$5 billion paying Ukrainians to riot and dismantle their democratically elected government." (https://www.politifact.com/factchecks/2014/mar/19/facebook-posts/united-states-spent-5-billion-ukraine-anti-governm/).

15. "Canadian embassy used as safe haven during Ukraine uprising, investigation finds," *CBC News*, July 12, 2015 (https://www.cbc.ca/news/politics/canadian-embassy-used-as-safe-haven-during-ukraine-uprising-investigation-finds-1.3148719).

16. "Chernivtsi Hosts Groundbreaking Canadian Studies Conference in Ukraine" (http://www.infoukes.com/newpathway/22-2010-Page-8-1.html),

17. Nash Holos, Ukrainian Roots Radio (http://www.nashholos.com/audio/Podcast-Interview-2014-0202-Inna_Tsarkova.mp3).

18. Allen Ruff, "What the Mainstream Misses: Observations on the Ukraine Crisis," *Huffington Post*, Apr. 1, 2014 (https://www.huffpost.com/entry/what-the-mainstream-misse_b_5063302).

19. Ivan Katchanovski, "The Far Right in Ukraine During the 'Euromaidan' and Beyond," Conference: Annual Conference of the Canadian Association of Slavists, May 2015.

20. "Canada Condemns Use of Force Against Protesters in Ukraine," Global Affairs Canada, Nov. 30, 2013 (https://www.international.gc.ca/media/aff/news-communiques/2013/11/30a.aspx?lang=eng).

21. "Canada's Foreign Minister, the Honourable John Baird visits the 'Maidan' in Kyiv, Ukraine," Ukrainian Canadian Congress, Dec. 5, 2013 (https://www.ucc.ca/2013/12/05/news-canadas-foreign-minister-the-honourable-john-baird-visits-the-maidan-in-kyiv-ukraine/).

22. "Winter on Fire: Ukraine's Fight for Freedom," Netflix, Documentary 2015.

23. "Ukraine's Viktor Yanukovych urged to respect pro-EU protests," *CBC News*, Dec. 5, 2013 (https://www.cbc.ca/news/world/ukraine-s-viktor-yanukovych-urged-to-respect-pro-eu-protests-1.2451728).

24. "Ukraine-Russia deal is bad for Canada," *Ottawa Citizen*, Jan. 7, 2014.

25. "Why is a 'heroine' of Ukraine's revolution charged with murder?," *Al Jazeera*, Apr. 17, 2020 (https://www.aljazeera.com/features/2020/4/17/why-is-a-heroine-of-ukraines-revolution-charged-with-murder).

26. "Harper says Ukraine leaning to Soviet past, condemns violence," Canadian Press, Jan. 27, 2014 (https://www.cp24.com/

news/harper-says-ukraine-leaning-to-soviet-past-condemns-violence-1.1658182).

27. "Canada expands sanctions on Ukraine's Viktor Yanukovych, officials," *CBC News*, Feb. 20, 2014 (https://www.cbc.ca/news/politics/canada-expands-sanctions-on-ukraine-s-viktor-yanukovych-officials-1.2545140).

28. Ivan Katchanovski, op. cit.

29. Ibid.; "Ukraine Maidan deaths: Who fired shots?," *BBC News*, Feb. 12, 2015 (https://www.bbc.com/news/av/world-europe-31435719).

30. "Ukraine crisis: Transcript of leaked Nuland-Pyatt cal," *BBC News*, Feb. 7, 2014, (https://www.bbc.com/news/world-europe-26079957).

31. Irvin Studin, "Does Canada really care about Ukraine?" *The Toronto Star*, Apr. 11, 2014; James Fitz-Morris, "John Baird in Ukraine while Ottawa holds off on sanctions," *CBC News*, Feb. 27, 2014.

32. David Morrison, "Why the Ukraine regime is wholly illegitimate," Apr. 18, 2014 (www.david-morrison.org.uk/ukraine/why-ukrainian-regime-illegitimate.htm).

33. Jessica Hume, "John Baird in Ukraine to meet new gov't," *The Toronto Sun*, Feb, 27 2014.

34. "Baird calls Russian moves 'provocative' as he meets with new Ukraine government officials," *The Toronto Sun*, Feb, 28 2014.

35. Susana Mas, "Ukraine to get $220M in financial support from Canada," *CBC News*, Mar. 13, 2014.

36. "Foreign Minister John Baird to lead Canadian delegation to Ukraine," *CTV News*, Calgary, Feb. 25, 2014.

37. "Stephen Harper in Kyiv as first G7 leader to stand beside new Ukraine government," *The National Post*, Mar. 22, 2014.

38. Tim Harper, "Stephen Harper has harsh words for Putin on historic visit to Ukraine," *The Toronto Star*, Mar. 22, 2014.

Brazil, 2016

1. Jonathan Watts, "Brazil minister ousted after secret tape reveals plot to topple President Rousseff," *The Guardian*, May 23, 2016.

2. Natalia Viana, Rafael Neve, "Brazil: The FBI and Lava Jato," (https://lab.org.uk/brazil-the-fbi-and-lava-jato/).

3. "Canada to Continue Advancing Common Ties With Brazil Amid Impeachment", Sep. 2, 2016 (https://sputniknews.com/politics/201609021044874721-canada-brazil-ties-impeachment/).

4. "Joint statement on the launch of negotiations toward a comprehensive free trade agreement between Canada and the Mercosur member states," Mar. 9, 2018 (https://www.international.gc.ca/trade-commerce/trade-agreements-accords-commerciaux/agr-acc/mercosur/joint_statement-declaration_commune.aspx?lang=eng).

5. "Third Canada-Brazil Strategic Partnership Dialogue to be held in Ottawa," Global Affairs Canada, News release, Oct. 22, 2018.

6. "Brazil's Lula Leaves Office With 83% Approval Rating, Folha Says," Dec. 19, 2010 (https://www.bloomberg.com/news/articles/2010-12-19/brazil-s-lula-leaves-office-with-83-approval-rating-folha-says).

7. "Brazilian general sets country on edge by hinting of military intervention if courts rule in favour of former president," *The Globe and Mail*, Apr. 4, 2018.

8. Caroline Orr, "It turns out Trudeau wasn't snubbed by Bolsonaro," *Canada's National Observer*, July 5, 2019.

9. Chris Arsenault, "What a far-right Bolsonaro presidency in Brazil means for Canadian business," *CBC News*, Oct. 26, 2018.

10. Ibid.

Bolivia, 2019

1. "How an Unknown Female Senator Came to Replace the Bolivian President Evo Morales," *The New York Times*, Nov. 24, 2019.

2. "Bolivia interim gov't proposes election bill as death toll mounts," Nov. 21, 2019 (https://www.aljazeera.com/news/2019/11/bolivia-interim-gov-proposes-election-bill-death-toll-mounts-191120222432439.html).

3. "Media Censorship & OAS' Participation in Election Process May Ruin Bolivia's Democracy," *Sputnik News*, Jan. 15, 2020.

4. Kepa Artaraz, *Bolivia: Refounding the Nation* (Pluto Press, 2012), 2.

5. Manny Moreno, "Bolivian opposition declares Pachamama unwelcome in palace," *Wild Hunt*, Nov 12, 2019 (https://wildhunt.org/2019/11/bolivian-opposition-declares-pachamama-un-welcome-in-palace.html)

6. "The bible makes a comeback in Bolivia with Jeanine Añez," *Open Democracy*, Nov. 20, 2019 (https://www.opendemocracy.net/en/democraciaabierta/.

7. "Canada welcomes results of OAS electoral audit mission to Bolivia," Global Affairs Canada, Nov. 10, 2019.

. Evan Dyer, "Canada calls for new vote after disputed Bolivian election," *CBC News*, Oct. 29, 2019.
9. Ibid.
10. "Prime Minister Justin Trudeau speaks with the President of Chile, Sebastián Piñera," Oc. 29, 2019 (https://www.pm.gc.ca/).
11. "Bolivia dismissed its October elections as fraudulent. Our research found no reason to suspect fraud," *The Washington Post*, Feb. 27, 2020.
12. "A Bitter Election. Accusations of Fraud. And Now Second Thoughts," *The New York Times*, June 7, 2020.
13. "Bolivia's Morales resigns amid scathing election report, rising protests," *The Washington Post*, Nov. 10, 2019.
14. Special Meeting of the Permanent Council, Nov. 12, 2019 (https://www.youtube.com/watch?v=KklG3V3PZTQ&feature=youtu.be).
15. "Morales lost Bolivia after shock mutiny by police," Reuters, Nov. 14, 2019.
16. Special Meeting of the Permanent Council, Nov. 12, 2019 (https://www.youtube.com/watch?v=KklG3V3PZTQ&feature=youtu.be).
17. "Canada and the US 'Ministry of Colonies,'" *People's Voice*, Nov. 13, 2019.
18. "Canada welcomes results of OAS electoral audit mission to Bolivia," Global Affairs Canada, Nov. 10 2019.
19. Canada at the OAS, Aug, 11, 2020,Twitter, Canada at the OAS, @CanadaOAS.
20. Cheryl Urban, Aug 6, 2020, Twitter, @cheryl_urban (https://publish.twitter.com/?query=https%3A%2F%2Ftwitter.com%2Fcheryl_urban%2Fstatus%2F1291399861087150081&widget=Tweet).

Peru, 2022
1. "Perú on the Lima Group: 'The Most Disastrous Thing We Have Done in International Politics,'" *The Orinoco Tribune*, Aug. 5, 2021.
2. "Peru's President: 2nd Agrarian Reform seeks to achieve food security and rural development," Oct. 17, 2022 (https://andina.pe/ingles/).
3. Yves Engler, "Ottawa backs removal of elected Peruvian president despite protests," Dec. 15, 2022 (https://springmag.ca/ottawa-backs-removal-of-elected-peruvian-president-despite-protests).
4. Vijay Prashad and José Carlos Llerena Robles, "The US Egged on the Coup in Peru," Dec. 15, 2022 (https://alborada.net/castillo-coup-washington-embassy-fujimori/).

5. Louis Marcotte, Dec. 14, 2022 (https://twitter.com/louiscmarcotte/status/1603185345377587200).

6. "Canada takes sides as hemisphere splits over who rules Peru," *CBC News*, Dec. 16, 2022.

7. "State Secretary reiterates U.S. support for Peru's Government," Dec. 17, 2022 (https://andina.pe/Ingles/).

8. "Canada takes sides as hemisphere splits over who rules Peru," *CBC News*, Dec. 16, 2022.

9. "Peru's Oligarchy Overthrows President Castillo," Dec. 11, 2022 (https://alborada.net/peru-castillo-coup-oligarchy/).

Venezuela, 2017 to the Present

1. Greg Shupak, "US Media Erase Years of Chavismo's Gains," *Fair*, Feb. 20, 2019 (https://fair.org/home/us-media-erase-years-of-chavismos-gains/).

2. "Venezuela: Social Program Meets Goal, Delivers 3 Million Homes," *TeleSur English*, Dec. 27, 2019 (https://www.telesurenglish.net/news/).

3. Tamara Pearson, "Municipal Election Results: Venezuela Winning the War Waged against It," *Venezuela Analysis*, Dec. 9, 2013 (https://venezuelanalysis.com/analysis/10232).

4. "U.S. declares Venezuela a national security threat, sanctions top officials," Reuters, Mar. 9, 2015.

5. "Trump repeatedly suggested Venezuela invasion, stunning top aides – report," *The Guardian*, July 5, 2018.

6. "Venezuela makes six arrests in alleged Maduro assassination attempt," *CNN*, Aug. 6, 2018.

7. "Canada condemns Venezuela's 'undemocratic' vote but is not ready to follow U.S. sanctions yet," *Radio Canada International*, July 31, 2017.

8. "Venezuela: Six States Request ICC Investigation," Human Rights Watch, Sept. 26, 2018 (https://www.hrw.org/news/2018/09/26/venezuela-six-states-request-icc-investigation).

9. Daniel Joloy, "Ten years of militarised drug policies in Mexico: more violence and human rights violations," May 7, 2017 (https://www.opendemocracy.net/en/ten-years-of-militarised-drug-policies-in-mexico-more-violence-and-human-rights-violati/).

10. "Prime Minister Justin Trudeau speaks with President of Peru, Pedro Pablo Kuczynski," May 1, 2017 (https://pm.gc.ca/en/news/).

11. "Statement of the fifth meeting of the Lima Group on the situation in Venezuela, Spanish version," Global Affairs Canada, Feb. 13, 2018; Yves Engler, "Ottawa is trying to interfere in Venezuela's election," Apr. 1, 2018 (https://rabble.ca/blogs/bloggers/yves-englers-blog/2018/04/ottawa-trying-interfere-venezuelas-election).

12. Ibid.

13. "Lima Group rules out military intervention in Venezuela," Sept. 17, 2018 (https://www.aljazeera.com/news/2018/09/lima-group-rejects-military-intervention-venezuela-180917061724188.html); "Canada, Latin American allies at odds over Venezuela intervention pledge," CBC News, Sep. 19, 2018.

14. "Canada's recognition of Juan Guaido as true Venezuelan leader was months in the making," Global News, Jan. 26, 2019; "Freeland spoke to Venezuelan opposition leader two weeks before he declared himself interim president, source says," Jan. 24, 2019.

15. "Anti-Maduro coalition grew from secret talks," Jan. 25, 2019 (https://apnews.com/d548c6a958ee4a1fb8479b242ddb82fd).

16. "Is Trudeau's Venezuela policy the Monroe Doctrine reborn?," The Canadian Dimension, Feb. 20, 2019.

17. "Prime Minister Justin Trudeau speaks with Prime Minister Pedro Sánchez of Spain," May 9, 2019 (https://pm.gc.ca/en/news/).

18. "Prime Minister of Canada announces closer collaboration with Japan," Apr. 28, 2019 (https://pm.gc.ca/en/news/).

19. Peter Zimonjic, "Lima Group embraces Venezuelan opposition leader Guaido, calls on military to quit Maduro," CBC News, Feb. 4, 2019.

20. "Venezuelans are forced to fight on, alone, against Maduro; Something big was happening in the broken country this week," The Ottawa Citizen, May 1, 2019.

21. Angus Berwick, Vivian Sequera, Corina Pons, Mayela Armas, Deisy Buitrago, and Luc Cohen, "Chaos in the streets as Venezuela's Guaido launches military uprising to oust Maduro," Reuters, Apr. 30, 2019 (https://globalnews.ca/news/5220106/venezuela-military-coup-juan-guaido/).

22. May 1, 2019 (https://twitter.com/cafreeland/status/1123758508573372417); "Canada requests emergency meeting of Lima Group to discuss Venezuela," Reuters, Apr. 30, 2019 (http://news.trust.org/item/20190430181904-9uqf2/).

23. Guaido calls for more street protests Apr. 30, 2019 (https://apnews.com/1b271ef1f15940f394343dd2027a23e2).

24. "Interim President of Venezuela Juan Guaidó to visit Canada," Prime Minister's Office, Jan. 26. 2020 (https://www.newswire.ca/news-releases/interim-president-of-venezuela-juan-guaido-to-visit-canada-830507706.html).

25. David Ljunggren, "Canada to impose sanctions on Venezuela's Maduro and top officials," Sep. 22, 2017 (https://ca.reuters.com/article/topNews/idCAKCN1BX2PV-OCATP).

26. Evan Dyer, "Canada expands Venezuela sanctions, adds 43 people close to Maduro," *CBC News*, Apr. 15, 2019 (https://www.cbc.ca/news/politics/venezuela-sanctions-canada-1.5098288).

27. "Venezuela accuses Canada of supporting Trump's 'war adventure'," AFP, Apr. 16, 2019 (https://www.france24.com/en/20190416-venezuela-accuses-canada-supporting-trumps-war-adventure).

28. Mark Weisbrot and Jeffrey Sachs, "Economic Sanctions as Collective Punishment: The Case of Venezuela," April 2019 (http://cepr.net/publications/reports/economic-sanctions-as-collective-punishment-the-case-of-venezuela).

29. Rahmat Mohamad, "Unilateral Sanctions in International Law: A Quest for Legality, Economic Sanctions under International Law," Mar. 4, 2015 (https://link.springer.com/chapter/10.1007%2F978-94-6265-051-0_4); *TeleSur English*, "UN Human Rights Council Condemns Sanctions Against Venezuela," Mar. 26, 2018 (https://venezuelanalysis.com/news/13737).

30. Ibid.

31. Telesur, "Trudeau Endorses Trump: Canadian Sanctions against Venezuela Violate 'International Law'," June 3, 2018 (https://www.globalresearch.ca/trudeau-endorses-trump-canadian-sanctions-against-venezuela-violate-international-law/5642871).

32. Michelle Carbert, "Canada encouraged diplomats to defend human rights in Venezuela," *The Globe and Mail*, July 16, 2018.

33. Peter Hum, "Choosing danger," *The Ottawa Citizen*, Aug. 19 2017.

34. Government Response to the July 2017 Report of the Standing Senate Committee on Foreign Affairs and International Trade: The Deepening Crisis in Venezuela: Canadian and Regional Stakes, Mar. 19, 2018.

35. Foreign Affairs, Trade and Development Canada, Government of Canada, Catalogue Number: FR2-16E-PDF, International Standard Serial Number (ISSN): 2368-5778, Departmental Performance Report 2014-15 (https://www.international.gc.ca/gac-amc/publications/plans/dpr-rmr/dpr-rmr_1415.aspx?lang=eng).

36. Ramón Antonio Pérez, Venezuela, "La dura denuncia de un jesuita sobre la violación de los DDHH," *Aleteia*, Sept. 22, 2017 (https://es.aleteia.org/2017/09/22/venezuela-la-dura-denuncia-de-un-jesuita-sobre-la-violacion-de-los-ddhh/).

37. "Embassy of Canada and the Center for Peace and Human Rights announce a call for the 8th edition of the Human Rights Award in Venezuela" (https://www.canadainternational.gc.ca/venezuela/highlights-faits/2016/2016-11-8thHRA_PDP.aspx?lang=eng).

38. Valentina Rodríguez Rodríguez, "Director de Codevida gana premio Derechos Humanos que otorga embajada de Canadá," *TalCual*, Mar. 7. 2018 (https://talcualdigital.com/director-de-codevida-gana-premio-derechos-humanos-que-otorga-embajada-de-canada/).

39. Francisco Valencia, director de Codevida, "Estamos frente a un Estado criminal," *Crisis en Venezuela* (https://crisisenvenezuela.com/project/entrevista-francisco-valencia-codevida-estamos-frente-un-estado-criminal/).

40. Michelle Carbert, "Venezuelan human-rights advocate applauds Canada's leadership in denouncing Nicolas Maduro regime," *The Globe and Mail*, July 4, 2018.

41. "Antonio Ledezma pidió en Canadá intervención humanitaria para rescatar a Venezuela," *Diario Las Américas*, Sep. 20 2018 (https://www.diariolasamericas.com/america-latina/antonio-ledezma-pidio-canada-intervencion-humanitaria-rescatar-venezuela-n4162779).

42. Ibid.

43. Rachael Boothroyd Rojas, "Opposition Former Mayor Antonio Ledezma Breaks House Arrest, Flees to Colombia," *Venezuela Analysis*, Nov. 17, 2017 (https://venezuelanalysis.com/news/13506).

44. Tamara Pearson and Ryan Mallett-Outtrim, "Venezuelan Guarimbas: 11 Things the Media Didn't Tell You," Feb. 16, 2015 (https://venezuelanalysis.com/analysis/11211).

45. Popular Will (https://en.wikipedia.org/wiki/Popular_Will).

46. Ibid.

47. David Luhnow, Juan Forero and José de Córdoba, "'What the hell is going on?' How a tiny cabal galvanised Venezuela's Opposition," *Wall Street Journal*, Feb. 7, 2017.

48. "5 Things To Know About Venezuela's Protest Leader, "*NPR*, Feb. 20, 2014 (https://www.npr.org/sections/thetwo-way/2014/

02/20/280207441/5-things-to-know-about-venezuelas-protest-leader).

49. Ibid.

50. Tamara Pearson and Ryan Mallett-Outtrim, "Venezuelan Guarimbas: 11 Things the Media Didn't Tell You," *Venezuela Analysis*, Feb. 16, 2015 (https://venezuelanalysis.com/analysis/11211).

51. Yves Engler, Canada's Trudeau Government Supportive of Venezuela Anti-democratic Hardline Elements, Global Research, May 31 2019 (https://www.globalresearch.ca/ottawa-anti-democratic-hardline-venezuelas-opposition/5679142).

52. Feb. 3, 2017 (https://twitter.com/voluntadPopular/status/827525918805598208).

53. Lucas Koerner, "Trump Meets with Venezuela's Lilian Tintori, Demands Release of Leopoldo Lopez," *Venezuela Analysis*, Feb. 16, 2017 (https://venezuelanalysis.com/news/12934); Joe Parkin Daniels, Tom Phillips and Sabrina Siddiqui, "This man plotted Guaidó's rise – and still dreams of leading Venezuela," *The Guardian*, Feb. 7 201).

54. Yves Engler, "Ottawa in bed with anti-democratic, hardline part of Venezuela's opposition," May 30, 2019, YvesEngler.com

55. Joe Parkin Daniels, Tom Phillips and Sabrina Siddiqui, "This man plotted Guaidó's rise – and still dreams of leading Venezuela," *The Guardian*, Feb. 7, 2019.

56. "'What the hell is going on?' How a tiny cabal galvanised Venezuela's Opposition," *Wall Street Journal*, Feb. 7, 2019.

57. Allan Culham, "Venezuela, after midnight," *Open Canada*, May 24, 2016 (https://www.opencanada.org/features/venezuela-after-midnight/).

58. DAS DESHAZO'S MEETING WITH AMBASSADORS ON 2/16/2004, Canonical ID:04CARACAS628_a (https://wikileaks.org/plusd/cables/04CARACAS628_a.html).

59. Maria Corina Machado (https://en.wikipedia.org/wiki/Mar%C3%ADa_Corina_Machado).

60. "Canada's Foreign Service Awards Celebrate their 30th Year," June 14, 2019 (https://pafso.com/canadas-foreign-service-awards-celebrate-their-30th-year/).

61. Ibid.

62. Tyler Shipley, *Canada in the World*.

Conclusion

1. Shiri Pasternak, "Mercenary colonialism: Third-party management," *Ricochet*, Oct. 25, 2017 (https://ricochet.media/en/1994/mercenary-colonialism-third-party-management).

2. Shiri Pasternak, "They're Clear Cutting Our Way of Life,"ISSUE 8, Oct. 26, 2009 (https://uppingtheanti.org/journal/article/08-theyre-clear-cutting-our-way-of-life), (http://www.barrierelake-solidarity.org/2017/03/human-rights-delegates-to-barriere-lake.html).

3. Gale Courey Toensing, "Barriere Lake rallies for traditional governance and treaty rights," *Indian Country Today*, Dec. 24, 2010 (https://indiancountrytoday.com/archive/barriere-lake-rallies-for-traditional-governance-and-treaty-right).

4. "'Make the Economy Scream': Secret Documents Show Nixon, Kissinger Role Backing 1973 Chile Coup," *Democracy Now*, Sep. 10, 2013.

5. David C. Adams and Janet Rodriguez, "US tightens the screws on Venezuela's Maduro with banking sanctions," *Univision*, Mar. 22, 2019 (https://www.univision.com/univision-news/latin-america/us-tightens-the-screws-on-venezuelas-maduro-with-banking-sanctions).

6. Owen Schalk, " The Capitalist Roots of Anti-Indigenous Racism in Canada: Howard Adams' *Prison of Grass*," *Liberated Texts*, Nov. 22, 2021 (https://liberatedtexts.com/reviews/the-capitalist-roots-of-anti-Indigenous-racism-in-canada-howard-adams-prison-of-grass/).

7. Timothy David Clark, "Canadian Mining in Neo-Liberal Chile: Of Private Virtues and Public Vices," in *Community Rights and Corporate Responsibility: Canadian Mining and Oil Companies in Latin America* (Toronto: Between the Lines, 2006), 100.

8. Westphalian model (http://www.westarctica.wiki/index.php/Westphalian_model)

9. Robert Fife and Steven Chase, "Trudeau says he has no knowledge of China funding federal candidates, sidesteps questions of election interference," *The Globe and Mail*, Nov. 29, 2022.

MORE FROM BARAKA BOOKS

ARSENIC MON AMOUR
Letters of Love and Rag
Jean-Lou David & Gabrielle Izaguirré-Falardeau
(Translated by Mary O'Connor)

BUT WE BUILT ROADS FOR THEM
The Lies, Racism and False Memories
about Italy's Colonial Past
Francesco Filippi (Translated by Domenic Cusmano)

THE SEVEN NATIONS OF CANADA 1660-1860
Solidarity, Vision and Independence in the St. Lawrence Valley
Jean-Pierre Sawaya

THE LEGACY OF LOUIS RIEL
Leader of the Métis People
John Andrew Morrow

AFTER ALL WAS LOST
Resilience of a Rwandan Family Orphaned on Apr. 6 '94
When the Rwandan
President's Plane was Shot Down
Alice Nsabimana

ISRAEL: A BEACHHEAD IN THE MIDDLE EAST
From European Colony to US Power Projection Platform
Stephen Gowans

Printed by Imprimerie Gauvin
Gatineau, Québec